Architecture for the Arts The De Santos & Sicardi Galleries

BRAVE / ARCHITECTURE

De Santos Gallery

Sicardi Gallery

Architecture for the Arts The De Santos & Sicardi Galleries

BRAVE / ARCHITECTURE

Foreword
by Lars Lerup

Introduction
by Fernando Brave, FAIA

Epilogue
by Anna Mod

OSCAR RIERA OJEDA
PUBLISHERS

SICARDI GALLERY

Contents

Sicardi Gallery

Acknowledgements Fernando Brave

For this book, and the two building projects within, I owe gratitude to many. First on the list are the Owners of the De Santos Gallery, Luis and Gemma De Santos. These wonderful people gave me an incredible, once-in-a-lifetime opportunity when they hired my months-old firm to design their dream project. At the time, this was undoubtedly a dreamed project for me as well.

Maria Ines Sicardi, the founder of Sicardi Gallery, had been talking to me for a number of years about building her gallery. I thank her for introducing me to Luis and Gemma before she was ready to build her own gallery. Maria Ines is foremost a friend and a wonderful individual with whom I share, and have celebrated many birthdays. She is a visionary, someone who brought immeasurable art talent to the forefront. Maria Ines and her business partners Alison Ayers and Carlos Bacino were wonderful clients and continue to be delightful friends.

The Sicardi project would not have been the same without Joseph Helfenstein's endorsement. Maria Ines wanted to make sure he and the Menil Museum were happy with the design, and thought it fitting, as it sits across the street from their campus. The former Director at The Menil Foundation, who during a day in Houston with unusually pleasant weather walked from his museum office to our studio, reviewed the preliminary plans and gave it a thumbs-up.

Any acclaim earned for De Santos and Sicardi is shared with Eimar Virkus, of Virkus Construction, and Michael Scheurich and Mike Vaughn of Arch-Con Corporation. These companies succeeded in bringing to life what I could only put on paper.

The engineering consultants who collaborated on these projects were instrumental in making them a reality: Matrix Structural Engineers acted as the structural consultant for both projects. Chip Hurley (no longer with the firm) and Moyeen Haque always manage to handle my cantilever acrobatics, whatever the structural system or how challenging a construction budget may be. Curt Jones of Jones Engineers and Thom Kolupski of TKG & Associates were the MEP consultants that made all the fluids going back-and-forth in the veins of these two buildings come to life.

Many thanks go to my architectural collaborators on these two projects. For the De Santos Gallery, Terry J. Newton, AIA and Alejandro Brave. For the Sicardi Gallery, Alp Bozkurt, Bryant Alcantara and Alejandro Brave. I'd like to also thank Christian Sheridan, an integral part of our team and a long-time collaborator who proofed my writings for this book, and has edited the majority of my writing for more than ten years. The project drawings in this book were prepared by long-time collaborator Peter Ho, AIA (plans, sections, elevations), and my brother and multiple-project associate Alejandro Brave (axonometrics).

Bookending this volume are Lars Lerup's insightful Foreword and Anna Mod's on-point Epilogue. For capturing in words the essence of my work, I am indebted to them both.

Appreciation also goes to the architecture awards juries of the AIA Houston and the Texas Society of Architects, which selected both projects for multiple awards. I would also like to honor the writers who wrote about Sicardi Gallery, including Ben Koush, AIA (Texas Architect, Arts + Culture), Helen B. Bechtel (OffCite.org), Whitney Radley (CultureMap Houston), Kelly Klaasmeyer (Swamplot) and, Catherine D. Anspon (Paper City). To the people who wrote about the De Santos Gallery including Val Glitsch, FAIA (Texas Architect), Iyna Bort Caruso (The Wall Street Journal), Linda Barth (Houston House & Home), Clifford Pugh (Houston Chronicle), and Tim Moloney (002 Magazine). To the wonderful Stephen Fox, who included both projects in the Third Edition of his Architectural Guide of Houston, published by the AIA Houston. To Wallpaper and to Phaidon for featuring Sicardi on City Guide of Houston and Destination Architecture Guide, respectively. To Aaron Seward, Editor of Texas Architect, who graciously provided the two articles reproduced in this book. And to Oscar Riera Ojeda who encouraged me to author it.

Of course, the photographers who through the justice of their cameras made these two projects look as good on the page as they do in real life: Paul Hester, Luis De Santos, Julie Pizzo Wood, and Rene Magdaleno.

Last, and of no minor relevance, I thank my wife Marcela Descalzi who encourages me on my many pursuits, architecturally or otherwise, and my children, Ivan, Axel, Alana, and Anouk whose freshness, intelligence, and spirit of adventure accompany me wherever I go.

Foreword Lars Lerup

Beating the Tin Drum on High Street

Tin is the local shorthand for architecture in the city of Houston. This is a material choice of surprising intelligence and foresight. Houston, a city of a certain infamy stemming from No Zoning, Endless Sprawl, Paved Bayous, Invisible Ozone, and all of this enhanced only by Space Programs, Wars on Cancer, and occasional corporate showstoppers built by well-known architects. How does a young generation of architects, burdened with a decent education and debt to match, establish its presence in such a sea of housie-houses, big-box stores, and strip malls? Not by individual expression, but instead by unspoken agreement, by shared expression, by camaraderie, by collusion. By selecting a humble material drawn from the manufacturing and storage backwaters of the city. And, in choosing this material, by signaling that we draw our inspiration from sprawl itself, from endless repetition, unrelenting sameness, from states of frugality and circumstances of limited funding. As explored by historians Drexel Turner, Stephen Fox, and Ben Koush, Houston's "tin drum" was first played by Howard Barnstone in his Art Barn of 1969.

Barnstone's deployment of tin at Rice University, a place then blindly committed to St. Joe brick, was a move of distinct brilliance. Not only did the project rebel against the brick establishment but it also brought tin to one of the state's most celebrated places of higher education, cleverly reclaiming material that had been consigned to the conceptual dustbin. Sprawl had come to campus.

De Santos Forty-five years later tin has moved to High Street in the hands of Fernando Brave and his two clients, gallerists Luis de Santos (2003) and, more recently, Maria Ines Sicardi (2012). The De Santos Gallery has since changed ownership and use, so we will limit ourselves to its outside. The Sicardi is still going full steam and working from its space we will expand the scope of our reflection to consider how modern architecture has transcended the building.

The ten-year time difference between the two gallery projects illustrates a design "leap" built upon the same grammatical premise. The first gallery represents

the Brave design apparatus in its fullest expression, a mode often typical of early careers and not always the most effective. In Brave's mind his tripartite use of materials—the signature, tin, and then stucco and glass— signals an exterior expression of the interior. But the materials themselves are overcome by form. Blocks of space, nested and discrete, are stacked in contradistinction to the flat box culture that surrounds it. The project's formal ambition is enhanced and marked by its three materials. A hierarchy emerges—tin claims its status by covering the gallery space, while the support boxes are designed in stucco. Glass, the third material, divides and differentiates the blocks of space.

The top of the stack of blocks is not the common pitched roof but rather a flat surface and, in the case of both galleries, a terrace. The terrace compensates for the ground lost to the footprint of the gallery and offers additional entertainment space at gallery openings. In some ways the terrace and flat roof seem perfectly suited to Houston, a city of perpetual flooding—a flat roof can be fashioned such that it retains water rather than allowing it to rush it into the street. But such water-retaining measures have never been adapted in the city because of a fear of leaks, among other things.

In the end, Brave's stacking transports the gallery's occupants to the tree canopy and offers a momentary relief from the bustle of the city.

Sicardi the later gallery project propels both Brave's work and the state of architecture, and its relation to art, in Houston. Location is a mysterious conundrum in a place without hierarchies and in a city characterized by what seems an instant amnesia, here, strangely, history plays a role. Richmond Avenue, for example, is a long street with a history of nowforgotten modern architecture; a few lonely markers reminiscent of Le Corbusier's Villa Savoy remain. Along Richmond closer to Montrose, the cardo[1] of the Museum district, the border of the frazzled lesser edge of the Menil Foundation begins to expand the cultural network already anchored by two museums. The parallel West Alabama Street, which lines the Menil's front edge and marks the opening to its spectacular campus, takes on the role of the decumanus. So where does Maria Ines Sicardi locate her gallery? Right across the street! It is a demanding location—according to Aristotle "you should never mention yourself in the company of the greats" unless, as in this case, you are in fact one of them. Indeed, Sicardi has built a compelling venue for South American art and a challenging partner to Menil—a perfect project for Fernando Brave.

Renzo Piano's calm rectitude of well-lit space furnished by broad hall, white walls, an intelligent ceiling sits heavily on the design of museum space in Houston and around the world. Brave's Sicardi meets the challenge posed by this convention. Although architects (still) prefer their buildings -sans-humans there is in truth no way to break up the triangulation of space, art, and its kibitzers. The Sicardi gallery proves this eloquently. As one walks through the majestic ground-floor space, sixteen-foot ceilings move the space from the mundane to the poetic. Add to this the art itself. Just as material and craftsmanship are understood to form built space, so art and its mesmerized beholder make architecture, now in time. Indeed, here architecture is no longer just the built but is, too, a collusion of humans and our nonhuman partners. Like trees falling in the forest, buildings need a world, need witness, to exist. It is hard to find a worthier partner in this than art and its aficionados.

In the Sicardi space, the commercial operations of the art world are laid bare but somehow now without the vulgarities (and reality) of the market. The result is an open plan with a series of white rooms that blend together the "served" and "serving" spaces that at the Menil are strictly demarcated. At Sicardi, the traditional narrative internal to the gallery's exhibitions is discarded in favor of a new openness. The implied distance between the viewer and the art is erased. A long stair that takes us up to a second floor is lit by and oriented along a large window visible from West Alabama. Here, again, the galleries merge with the support space. At one gap the exterior boxes are suddenly felt and we can escape onto a wooden deck. On the deck we are suddenly exactly proximate to the boxes, suddenly intimate with their materiality.

On "West Alabama," a street that seems worthy of a song, the Menil is behind us and the stacked blocks reappear. Here the stuccoed bottom block, visibly burdened by the wide striations of the tin siding, is only broken by the square stair-window that stares, Cyclopic, down at us. If the Menil Foundation is the queen of Houston's art world, surely other dignitaries occupy other streets in the district, anchoring the Museum District along the bottom of the cardo. Sicardi stands out against these other private galleries, remarkable not only in its deliberate position on the decumanus next to the Menil but also in its understated elegance and powerful commitment to the highest quality of exhibition. The gallery has dared to present itself—not only as architecture against the dull sameness of the sprawling city but also as a worthy companion to the celebrated museum. The two, now in tandem, rattle the everyday.

Footnote

[1] *refer here to the Roman organization of the city along two crossing axes—the cardo and the decumanus—with the aim of suggesting that even in a highly unplanned city like Houston some organization of activity takes place. This occurred, in the past, along streets known colloquially as strips. This curious similarity is, I suggest, beginning to define the generally loose conception of the Museum District.*

Lars Lerup

Lars Lerup is the Albert K and Harry K Smith Professor of Architecture and Dean Emeritus of Rice University School of Architecture. He is an emeritus professor at the College of Environmental Design at UC Berkeley. He is an author of several books, *Building the Unfinished: Architecture and Human Action* (1977), *Planned Assaults* (1987), *After the City* (2001), *One Million Acres and No Zoning* (2011), *The Continuous City* (2017) and numerous articles. His books have been published in English, Chinese and German. He was elected Swedish American 2004 byVasa Orden and the Arnold W. Brunner Rome Prize Fellow at the American Academy in Rome 2009-2010.

Introduction Fernando Brave

'Creativity requires the courage to let go of certainties' — Erich Fromm

Two Galleries in Context

My relocation to Houston appears to coincide with the dusk of two great decades of architecture in the city. Architectural Historian Stephen Fox declared that in the 1970's and 80's the city lived through a significant architectural peak[1]. The buildings constructed during those years placed Houston among one of the world's best examples of architecture. It is safe to assume that the opening of the Menil Collection (fig.1) building just three days before my arrival to Houston influenced the way I began to assimilate the city.

fig 1. The Menil Collection, Renzo Piano

I was awe-struck by personally experiencing the buildings I had only seen in print as an architecture student, including Philip Johnson's Pennzoil Place (fig.2), James Wines' Indeterminate Façade for the electronics chain store BEST (fig.3), Roche-Dinkeloo's Conoco Headquarters (fig.4), a few buildings by Arquitectonica (fig.5), the Rothko Chapel (in which I eventually got married) (fig.6), and others. The microclimate of more subdued local architecture trends was also moving. Lars Lerup could not have been more precise when he wrote that "contemporary Houston is neither city nor metropolis, but an urban condition of a third kind."[2] The contrast between the much denser Buenos Aires, where I had come from, and the automobile-centric Houston (fig.7) could not have had a greater impact in me. It guided the process by which I gradually discovered, and in parallel understood, the city.

fig 2. Pennzoil Place, Philip Johnson & John Burgee

While exploring the city to foundationally build on my newfound Houston rootedness[3], I was quickly drawn to the restrained, corrugated metal architecture of Howard Barnstone and Eugene Aubrey for the Dominique De Menil-backed buildings at Rice University, the Media Center and the Art Barn (fig.8). These two influential buildings are likely precedents for the metal-clad building designed by Gunnar Birkerts for the Contemporary Arts Museum (fig.9), completed in 1972. I also dis-covered a house designed by Aubrey in the Rice

fig 3. Indeterminate Façade, James Wines/SITE

fig 4. Conoco Headquarters, Kevin Roche & John Dinkeloo

fig 5. Townhomes in Houston, Arquitectonica

fig 6. Rothko Chapel, Howard Barnstone

fig 7. Houston, Texas

fig 8. Rice Art Barn, Howard Barnstone and Eugene Aubrey, 1969

fig 9. Contemporary Arts Museum in Houston, Gunnar Birkerts, 1972

Military neighborhood for an art dealer in 1974 (fig.10), which years later spurred the local Tin House movement. The Tin Houses of Houston, mostly built between the 1980's and 90's, are characterized by simple rectangular planes, sloping roofs and corrugated steel cladding. They were inspired by metal warehouses and low-cost agrarian buildings found on the outskirts of Houston. One could speculate, moreover, that the lack of a clear demarcation between urban and rural in Houston fostered this penetration of an agrarian language, and its use as a form of expression in urban buildings - mostly residential, but also commercial and institutional. The movement was highlighted during a Rice Design Alliance architecture tour named Tin Houses which took place in the Rice Military neighborhood in 1994 (fig.11).

Aubrey's project cemented my intention of designing a corrugated metal house for my family (which I built) in 1996. Years before, my wife Marcela and I had purchased a lot a few blocks away from the Aubrey-designed house in Rice Military, which unbeknownst to me at the time, would become the epicenter of the Tin House movement.[4] My interest in corrugated metal buildings started a decade earlier before beginning my architecture studies at the Universidad de Belgrano in Buenos Aires with

fig 10. The first Tin House, Eugene Aubrey, 1974

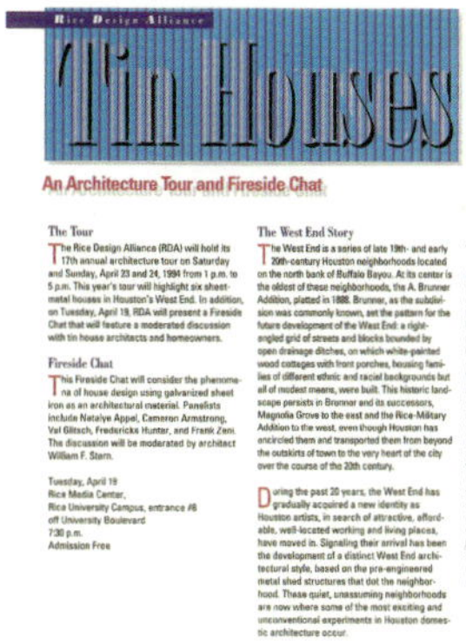

fig 11. Brochure for the Rice Design Alliance's 1994 Tin Homes Tour

fig 12. La Boca neighborhood, Buenos Aires

fig 13. Conventillo in La Boca, Buenos Aires

fig 14. Speaking about Sicardi and the "Rule of Threes" at the 2017 International Architecture Biennial in Buenos Aires

fig 15. My house in the Rice Military

the La Boca neighborhood (fig.12). Adjacent to the original port of the city of Buenos Aires, many European immigrants descended from transatlantic ships in search for a better life in the New World, mostly between the 1880's and the 1920's. The neighborhood is largely constructed of corrugated metal houses and tenement buildings, called conventillos[5] (fig.13), which to this day house the descendants of their resourceful builders.

Adhering to the (self-imposed) "Rule of Threes"[6] (fig.14) my house, shaped as a prism generated by extrusion and the simple repetition of the framing system elements, is clad in corrugated galvanized steel panels (tin), blue cement plaster, and glass (figs.15, 16, 17). Stemming from a ridiculously tight budget, my first solo project in the city has the intended (and humorous) simplicity of a doublewide trailer home. The "doublewide" sits on a more dignified rectangular plinth of blue plaster emphasizing the public side façade and the volume containing the common areas of the house, which open to the east. The corrugated metal of the second floor highlights the private rooms. The metal skin of the building drapes down to the ground plane on the west façade, behind which a spine containing service and utilitarian areas is placed. As pointed out by a writer, who paired the project to my family's

fig 16. My house in the Rice Military, Exterior detail

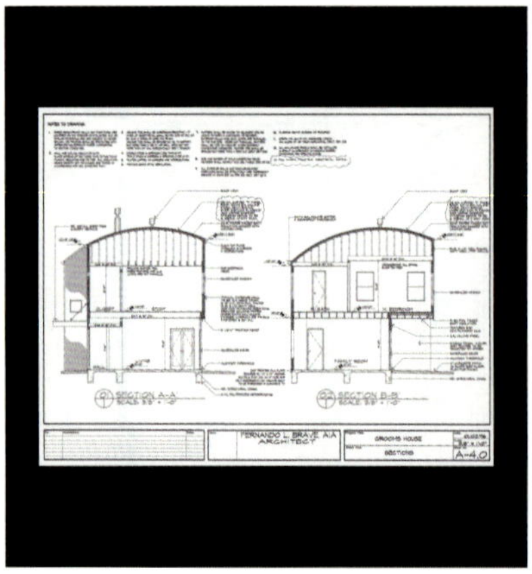

fig 17. My house in the Rice Military, Sections (before final roof modification)

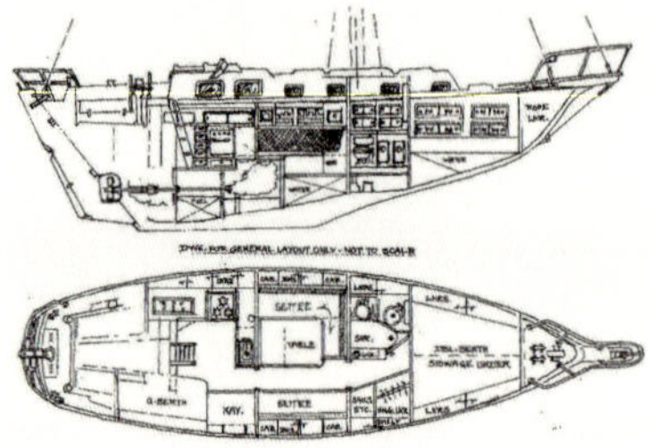

fig 18. Classic sailboat design with offset circulation

fig 19. As a 1st year architecture student in Buenos Aires

fig 20. Villino Tipo B – Roma, Adalberto Libera

fig 21. House with External Elevators, Antonio Sant'Elia

fig 22. Schminke House, Hans Scharoun

fig 23. Casa del Fascio, Giuseppe Terragni

fig 24. Novocomun Apartment, Giuseppe Terragni

"nautical pursuits" the house is organized along a single linear spine of circulation, placed off-center in plan - as one finds in sailboats (fig.18) as well as in the two galleries featured in this book.

Although my undergraduate architecture studies were in the midst of the postmodern movement, my eyes were focused elsewhere. During those years, I opted for a vertical studio (five years under the tutelage of a single head of studio) with strong rationalist influences (fig.19). Horacio Baliero[7], who once taught us that "pictures are not to be hanged on walls but rather should lean on one while sitting on a table, ledge, or the floor", was truly influential. Upon entering architecture school, I was immediately attracted to the work of Aalto, Kahn, Le Corbusier, Neutra, and van der Rohe. Delving beyond European rationalism, I discovered other movements that became very interesting to me including Italian Futurism, and Expressionism, as well as architects such as, Libera (fig.20), Mendelsohn, Sant'Elia (fig.21), Scharoun (fig.22), Schindler, and Terragni (figs.23, 24) to list a few. But Rationalism (fig.25) became a personal guiding light early on and remains so to the present day (fig.26). The movement is pivotal in architecture history. Its trailblazers radically transformed the practice of architecture, and with it, its meaning. Studying their work showed me not only how much influence these architects had received from their predecessors, but also how transformative and influential their work had become for those that followed them.

It became apparent to me that the compositional inclinations of the rationalists (with very few exceptions) had left behind potentially contributing elements of architecture such as color, texture, and drama (or the element of surprise). I find plenty of contemporary architecture to be not as crisp as that of the rationalists, modernists, or that of the international style that may have directly or indirectly inspired it. But what European Rationalists had in crispness and compositional clarity, they may have lacked in textural qualities. The work of Eero Saarinen was crucial in my discovery of the importance of texture as a fundamental element in

fig 25. Italian Rationalism: Colonia Fara Marine, Chiavari, Italy, 1936, Camillo Nardi Greco

fig 26. Exploring Rationalism with Texture, work as an architecture student, 1986

fig 27. Eero Saarinen's Dormitory at Yale University

composition. The cyclopean nature of his dormitory hall at Yale (fig.27), and what is achieved with a slight manipulation of the brick on the MIT Chapel's exterior walls (fig.28), both have outstanding textural merit. During one of my visits to the architecture library at my school in Buenos Aires, I came across an issue of Architectural Review featuring Glenn Murcutt's corrugated metal-clad Ball-Eastaway House (fig.29). This was the first time I noticed the use of such unassuming building material in custom residential architecture as a prime compositional element. The notion that this simple material had much to offer in terms of texture, and that it had fabulous potential to engage in dynamic dialogue with natural light crystalized for me at that moment.

One of my history professors, another modernist, referring to the "current state of affairs" (remember that I was in Architecture school during the boom of Postmodernism) once during a lecture I attended as a student said in passing, "...corremos peligro" (we are in danger) as if implying that if we let ourselves be carried away by ongoing architectural fashions, we might lose sight of where the truth in architecture lies - as if such a universal thing could ever be achieved (fig.30).

When observing the seeming lack of clarity in which architecture lies today, it is easy to think that previous generations operated under more clarity. And by this I don't mean to insinuate that the profession is somewhat degraded, but rather that globalization, combined with the ease of mobility and the instant availability of information and data (some good, some not-so), have created a world in which there is some level of confusion as to what is right and what is wrong, especially for our architecture students. It is interesting to note that I was born when only three billion people inhabited this planet. Today we have surpassed seven billion – all in just half a century. This demographic explosion combined with infrastructure and housing needs demanded a massive response. The ensuing result of that is the rapid spread of innumerable design trends within which one can easily get lost. However, it is also true that the apparent triumph of certain architectural movements of the past is more clearly seen once its contemporary trivial clutter has dissipated through the filter of time, giving way for the finest to rise up.

Construction, as a response to basic human needs, appears to have been easier in the dawn of time. When construction began to be assisted first by mechanics (ramps, pulleys and other devices, and systematized by industrialization), and later permeated by the arts, it became architecture. Mostly through the wish of most designers, architecture carries with it the illusion of permanence - there seems to be a constant quest on the part of architects (and some patrons) to achieve this ultimate objective. I believe, however, that buildings, like the art within them as in the case of the galleries that are the subject of this book, should be temporal and be bound by the frame of its significance within a defined period of time. I am sure many would disagree. But when I asked if he sometimes worried that his wood pop-up sculptures would deteriorate in time, the late Houston artist Lee Littlefield once told me that such deterioration was an expected and inherent quality of his work, and that in part, such deterioration was part of the life of the sculpture (fig.31). This has an undeniable parallel with the beauty one can find in the process of aging and the effects this has on the human body. The pyramids of Egypt and the Pantheon in Rome, the latter being my all-time favorite structure, are salient examples of their respective epochs. However, for evident reasons we would not desire all of their contemporary constructions, and those that happen in between those periods, to still be standing. There is a reason they are gone. They became obsolete. A few historical buildings like the pyramids and the Pantheon are good to have, and are today mere objects of admiration providing a glimpse into the past which has more to do with an anthropological need than with a functional one (fig.32). And the task of all architects is to fulfill the functional needs of their clients and patrons, not to provide future historical referents of a gone past.

The basic tenets of classical architecture are inherently present in all respectable works of architecture,

fig 28. Eero Saarinen's MIT Chapel

fig 29. Ball-Eastaway House, Glenn Murcutt, 1983

fig 30. Postmodern exploration as a student, History Class, 1984

fig 31. Lee Littlefield's work

fig 32. At the Pantheon, Rome, 2014

fig 33. Definition of space through the arrangement of organizational planes (study)

whether explicitly or not. For this reason, I consider it imperative to go to the roots when considering precedents to feed the design process and one's philosophical design drivers. However, it is not enough to resort to recent examples; one must go to the precedents that may have informed more recent ones. In this way, nothing is lost in a game of "broken telephone". While working on a new design we must ask ourselves who or what inspired the examples that nourish our design process. Behind my work there is always a search of form through the carving of simple prisms, the distribution of minimal compositional elements, and a basic materiality. The definition of space through the arrangement of organizational planes is also an area of exploration in my work (fig.33). But unlike the rationalists, I consider texture on a building's skin to have a requisite quality, one as sensual as that of the human skin. Likewise, openings and fenestration must not be considered only as a way to allow light or mere physical access into a building. Windows should not be considered plain compositional elements of assemblage, but rather essential organic components integral to every building. Comparably to the eyes in the human body, these openings are portals into the "soul" of the building. And some of these concepts are what I tried to keep exploring with my students over many years of teaching architecture design studios.

fig 34. Manipulated solids: Beach House in Galveston, Texas

fig 35. Carved Prism: Study for a High-rise Building

fig 36. Elephant Rock in Sardinia

fig 37. One of my carved rock studies

fig 38. Visiting Alvaro Siza's Serralves Museum in Porto, Portugal, 2017

fig 39. Lumière Noire, Luis Tomasello

fig 40. Abstract painting, Anatol Wladyslaw, 1950

fig 41. Chromatic Rhythms III, Alfredo Hlito, 1949, MOMA Collection

fig 42. Sicardi Gallery, Tin Architecture or Gray Box

I believe in doing architecture by reduction rather than by the addition of parts. I am not inspired by, or interested in, design by collaging or assemblage of compositional elements. What drives my design exploration is the simple manipulation of solids: stretching, pulling, extruding (fig.34). The drive to this approach, in my case, may serve to satisfy a primal, internal need (fig.35). Elephant Rock[8] in the island of Sardinia, a site I once took a detour to visit, is to me an early example of man's manipulation of solids to create practical space (fig.36). Up to that point, I had no idea that such a practice had ever taken place.

Years earlier I had produced a series of sketches of carved stones to investigate the idea of raw vs. manipulated elements, rough vs. smooth surfaces, and natural vs. intervened landscapes (fig.37). The parallel between the Elephant Stone and my rough drawings of carved stones was personally enlightening. During a recent visit to Alvaro Siza's Serralves Museum in Porto (fig.38), I saw an exhibit of work by artist Gordon Matta Clark. I was pleasantly surprised to see among his wonderful drawings a few sketches for an unrealized project also involving carved stones.

As I was referring earlier to the time when arts permeated construction and turned it into architecture, I would presume that my attraction to architecture stems from the combination of what I absorbed growing up: construction and the arts. Three generations of Braves before me were constructors. And like construction, art collecting has been in my family for generations. My great-grandfather was known for owning a few significant pieces of art, mostly paintings on canvas. His son, my grandfather, followed his footsteps with a few pieces of his own plus some passed down by his parents. My parents started collecting art more seriously than their predecessors during my grade school years. They amassed a limited, but cohesive collection of paintings mostly from Argentine artists from the 1920's to the 1970's. They often lament never having been successful at obtaining a most desirable painting by some Brazilian artist they admire, and whose name escapes me, to be passed down from my grandfather to them.

My taste for collecting arises from having visited innumerable galleries with my parents while they met with artists, gallerists and curators. It did help my quest for collecting that Marcela also comes from a family where art appreciation and collecting were a part of their life. I started collecting modest pieces immediately after getting married. Later on, we transitioned to acquiring fewer, but more important pieces by mostly non-figurative Latin American artists. I am fortunate to have spent the last many years in Houston where there are a cohort of first-class commercial art galleries and museums. Our personal collection of over one hundred pieces does include a few passed-down from my and my wife's families. But before collecting, I studied art and frequented exhibits as often as I could. The art that is most appealing to me has influenced my work both through observation and understanding, and through the influence it had over the architecture that stimulates me.

From the irreverence of Dadaism, to the use of popular imagery in Pop Art, to the renouncement of the unneeded in Minimalism, these movements provide a constant stimulant source for my work. In our office, we have an interesting collection of pieces acquired through time. We have also commissioned a few site-specific installations. Among some of the artists that fuel my work are Hélio Oiticica, Leon Ferrari, Luis Tomasello (fig.39), Anatol Wladyslaw (fig.40), and Alfredo Hlito (fig.41).

To return to the works in this book, I am often asked about their context. Context, in my view, is not static, but rather it is organic and dynamic. It is constantly being defined. I see contextualism not as the process of trying to fit in among neighboring buildings as much as I see it as the effort to fit in to what is going on in a given area from the viewpoint of time rather than from a physical aspect alone. Every project, even one that may appear to negate it, contributes to the context-making process. If being contextual can be defined as giving meaning to the various parts of a building through reference to its wider surroundings, I include in this mix not only buildings, but also streetscape, historical framework, and the area's impending outlook. The two buildings that arethe subject of this publication are set within the context of a city that goes beyond the built environment near them.

These two galleries represent each other's counterpoint at various levels. One is an early design - really the first commission my firm received soon after its inception. The other one is recent. One is light, the other one dark. One represents photographers exclusively; the other offers a mix of art media. Although both buildings stand within blocks from each other, one is on an eclectic and very active commercial avenue while the other building is on a quieter street, abutting a museum's campus. Like my house, both buildings have a simple generating diagram, make use of very simple materials and adhere to non-extravagant budgets. They also both adhere to the "Rule of Threes". They are the beginning and culmination of a thought process that led my firm through exploration, growth, and maturing.

It is possible that what began with influences of the Tin movement in the De Santos project may have morphed in the Sicardi project, ten years later, into what architect and architectural historian Ben Koush calls a Gray Box[9]. This emerging local architecture movement is in my opinion imbued with the genetic markers of Houston's Tin Architecture (fig.42).

When visiting the galleries with Lars, he pointed out how encouraging it was to see the aesthetic exploration begun with the design of these buildings continue through their use, as occupants reshape what visitors will encounter at every visit.

This symbiosis between building design and building use is not always possible, or even considered, with other architecture projects.

In closing, I think the "conservative"[10] nature attributed to one of these galleries has to do with the search for modern classicism with which I undertook these two projects. In any case, I take that as a compliment.

Footnotes

[1] Houston in the second decade of the 21st century suggests that the architectural epoch of the 1970's and 80's – the period of Pennzoil Place and the Menil Collection – was an exceptional highpoint in the city's history rather than marking the attainment of a permanent state of architectural grace. See Stephen Fox - The AIA Houston Architectural Guide, Third Edition

[2] Lars Lerup: A Million Acres and no Zoning

[3] From Erich Fromm, Rootedness is the need to establish roots and to feel at home again in the world. Productively, rootedness enables us to grow beyond the security of our mother and establish ties with the outside world. With a nonproductive strategy, in contrast, we become fixated and afraid to move beyond the security and safety of our mother or a mother substitute. From Wikipedia - Rootedness

[4] Once the Art Barn was in operation, these sorts of buildings — simple masses, clad entirely in corrugated metal — began to multiply. Built mostly by members of the art community in marginal neighborhoods, where deed restrictions had either never existed or had long since lapsed, these "Tin Houses" slowly became recognized as an architectural phenomenon by the 1990s. Fernando Brave, FAIA, was part of the wave. In 1994, he designed and built a Tin House for his family in Houston's West End, the epicenter of the movement. See Ben Koush, AIA - A Tin Gallery, Texas Architect 07/08 2014

[5] Conventillos are collective urban dwellings found in Buenos Aires and other Latin American cities. They consist of a house in which rooms are rented by a family or by a group of single men. They were prevalent in Buenos Aires in the late 1800's and early 1900's as a response to massive immigration of people with limited financial resources arriving mostly from Europe. Often, conventillos represented the adaptive late use of large residential houses in neighborhoods that had fallen in social status. They typically provided poor sanitary conditions due to overcrowding. In general, they were long rows of rooms organized around a central patio, with walls and ceiling finished in corrugated sheet metal, and with a wooden structure similar to balloon-frame. The word derives from the diminutive of the Spanish word Convento (Convent).

[6] The Rule of Threes means using no more than three different finish materials on the façade of any building (including glass). The breaking of such rule from time-to-time is necessary to, by contrast, justify the legitimacy of the same. The rule may have subconscious roots stemming from the Classical orders, fixed on the number three.

[7] Horacio Baliero (1927-2004), also known as Bucho, was an Argentine architect and educator, and a representative of the avant-garde Functionalist movement of Argentina in the 1950's. Some of his greatest works include the Cementerio Parque and the Cementerio Israelita in Mar del Plata, Argentina, and the Colegio Nuestra Señora de Luján at the Ciudad Universitaria de Madrid. In 2004, the latter was incorporated into the international registry of the DOCOMOMO (International Committee for DOcumentation and COnservation of buildings, sites and neighborhoods of the MOdern MOvement). The building was also designated as Architectural Heritage of the City of Madrid jointly by the Fundación Colegio Oficial de Arquitectos de Madrid, and the Fundación Caja Madrid.

[8] Roccia dell'Elefante is a large mass of trachyte (volcanic) stone found outside Castelsardo in the north of Sardinia, Italy. The rock is believed to have broken off from a larger formation uphill and to have rolled down to where it rests today. Through centuries of erosion the rock assumed what in the collective imagination appears to resemble a pachyderm. Also known as Sa Pedra Pertunta, the rock was later carved to form several Domus de Janas, a type of pre-Nuragic ceremonial chamber found in Sardinia which were carved out between 3400 and 2700 BC.

[9] Architect and architectural historian Ben Koush, AIA, proposes that "Sicardi Gallery stands as the latest exemplar of what could indeed be described as a locally inflected architectural practice, however marginal it may be", one which he calls Gray Boxes. He goes on to say that "the new Sicardi Gallery brings the trend to the present moment. From the street, it appears to be a two-story corrugated metal clad volume set on top of a one-story white-stucco ground floor. In reality, it is a two-story building with a very tall first floor that extends into the metal clad section with a lower-ceilinged second floor above. A large, glazed cut out in the main volume lights the main stair. The Sicardi building is the latest sign that, on the whole, the Gray Boxes design mode produces meaningful modern buildings that respond to the physical and cultural environment of this city. Instead of big, generic Bauhaus boxes, these self-effacing, gray buildings quietly assume their places and provide and intriguing example of a contextually and environmentally responsive architecture for Houston." See Ben Koush, AIA - Gray Boxes: "Sicardi Gallery's New Building Extends a 10-Year Trend", Arts + Culture - 06/2012

[10] "The new "Tin" Sicardi Gallery building strongly suggests that the now 45-year-old Tin Building movement remains viable in Houston. Its elegantly resolved design and level of craftsmanship indicate a refinement of the cheeky bravado of its inaugural buildings. However, whereas the first Tin Buildings resonated because they brought Houston's industrial vernacular into the language of art, the Sicardi Gallery's carefully composed, neo-modern elevations and graceful proportions begin to seem conservative." See Ben Koush, AIA - A Tin Gallery, Texas Architect 07/08 2014

De Santos Gallery

'Obviously on the same page architecturally, owner and architect orchestrated the result, and experiencing the building reveals that the permanent art is the building' — Val Glitsch, FAIA - Texas Architect 09 / 10 2005

Description

The De Santos Gallery is located on an important traffic artery and commercial strip in Houston's Montrose District. It sits within walking distance of one of the region's most important museums, The Menil Collection, and numerous other local cultural organizations. The site, a typical Houston residential lot of 50'x125', is placed within this eclectic urban setting. The gallery was conceived as a vessel to display, promote, archive and sell contemporary photographic works by artists from around the world.

According to its owner, the project's long-term viability was once threatened by the looming prospect of the expansion of the city's light rail system. After much public outcry and opposition, the pertinent transportation agency decided to indefinitely postpone construction of the Richmond Avenue line. It is difficult to assess what impact this could have had on the building beyond the short-term disruption to the gallery's operation and access during construction of the proposed rail line.

As the entrance to the gallery is approached, the building begins to reveal its content. This is purposely done to gradually awaken the intellectual curiosity of the visitor. Once inside, the visitor gets a glimpse of the sculpture garden's reflection pool. The level of privacy and intimacy increases as the visitor progressively moves sectionally higher, from floor to floor. Although display and workspaces interconnect and open to each other, the upper two floors can work independently from the gallery allowing both areas to be operated by different tenants. For this purpose, with two spaces for each possible tenant, the parking is split as well.

The three-story building's ground floor is open to the public and houses the main gallery, the ception area, and other support functions. More private working areas, the photography studio, a processing dark-room, and a kitchenette are located on the semi-private second floor. The third floor houses a loft apartment that opens onto an expansive terrace used for outdoor portrait photography and casual gatherings. The three floors are interconnected by a continuum of vertical and horizontal openings allowing for visual and functional connectivity.

The building's massing responds directly to the project's space program and the specific site constraints. Due to the compact size of the lot and the site orientation, the shape of the building is nearly a formulaic response to these conditions. Most of the public and living areas face east where they receive the morning's natural light. Service areas and vertical circulation are placed on the west side of the building and provide a thermal buffer as well as help darken the gallery during evening art showings.

Primary finish materials in this modestly-budgeted building are cement plaster, galvanized corrugated steel panels, and glass. Scorched marine plywood completes the top portions of the front and back glass walls that bookend the double-height lobby. To minimize and control sun exposure, sunshade canopy shelves are provided at these locations. Natural light is allowed in the building or controlled as-needed. The interior of the building is conceived as a blank canvas, a simple backdrop for the art to be exhibited. The walls are finished in sheetrock, placed over a substrate that permits the installation and removal of art without damaging the surfaces. Other interior finishes include sealed concrete and pine wood floors.

Commingling among other buildings of various types and functions, the De Santos Gallery is a suiting neighbor along the eclectic urban corridor in which it is placed.

Project Data

Project Size
4,200 SF

Lot Size
50′ x 125′

Project Location
Houston, Texas

Completed
2003

Architect
BRAVE / ARCHITECTURE

Project Team
Fernando L. Brave, FAIA
Terry J. Newton, AIA
Alejandro Brave

Consultants
Matrix Structural Engineers
Structural

Jones Engineers
MEP

General Contractor
Virkus Construction

Design Awards
Honor Award -
AIA Houston, 2005

Honor Award -
Texas Society
of Architects, 2005

De Santos Gallery by Val Glitsch, FAIA

Integrating art into the life of a community often requires its separation from the everyday. Experiencing that separation makes viewing the artful object possible in its own place: a space filled with only its own sound. Brave/Architecture's new project for the De Santos Gallery is such a place, a building insulated from the busy urban street along which it sits.

An early sketch of the floor plan (see next page) shows the architect's intention to close the building to the street, revealing only glimpses of the contents rather than exposing too much to the public. "This is purposely done to gradually awaken the intellectual curiosity of the visitor," says Fernando Brave, AIA. The entry space, publicly accessible from the east, is flanked by two outdoor areas that accommodate overflow during openings. Visually expanding the dimensions of the interior space, these provide a shady, cool welcome. Services are situated along the west side, shielding public spaces from the strong light and heat. Introducing a reflecting pool along the west gallery's edge accentuates the sensory experience in a private patio while allowing indirect sunlight to bounce into the gallery through low windows, permitting full-width flexibility for hanging art at the proper viewing height.

The second-floor plan works almost the same way. A circulation spine edges a large studio (sometimes used as additional gallery space) and aligns services on the west side of building, continuing the light and heat buffer vertically. A void over the lobby visually connects the two main interior spaces via a bridge.

At the top, a third-floor roof deck, adjacent to the living/rest space and hidden from a street perspective, allows a survey of the neighborhood from a safe distance where city noise is reduced and cars appear pleasantly diminished. Elevation sketches (opposite page) reveal how the exterior evolved to reinforce the intentionally private nature of the building. They also illustrate how the massing developed from a single-material silhouette shaped by internal requirements to become more carved, losing its earlier flatness. As built, vertical and horizontal elements interact as the inside pushes outward. Still, the exterior remains minimalist, a simple palette of stucco and metal siding. Sheet metal expresses the accessibility of public spaces, while cement stucco signifies the private areas impenetrable by the public. One needn't "over-intellectualize it to understand it," Brave says.

Brave credits the owners with much of the project's success. "They knew what they wanted," he says, "but they didn't tell me how to do it." Obviously on the same page architecturally, owner and architect orchestrated the result, and experiencing the building reveals that the permanent art is the building.

Val Glitsch, FAIA, practices architecture in Houston.

Essay published in Texas Architecture,
TSA Design Awards, Issue Number 55/05,
September/October 2005
www.texasarchitect.org

Sketches

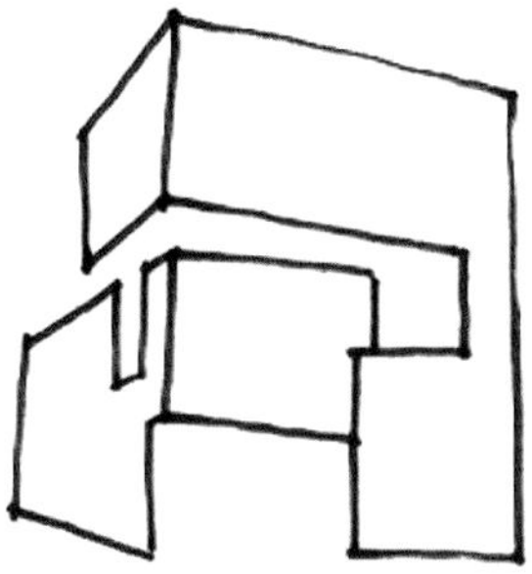

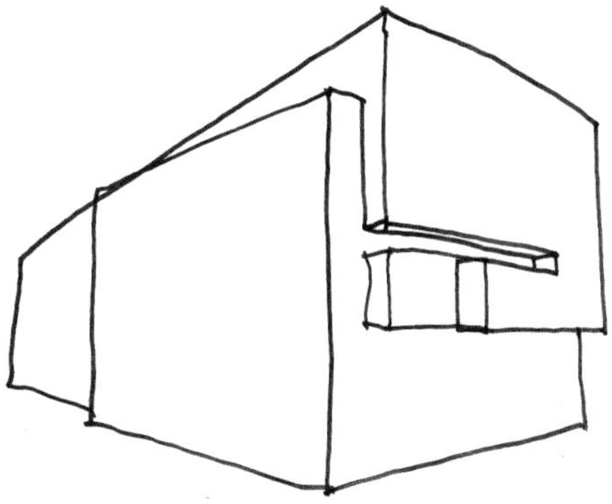

North A

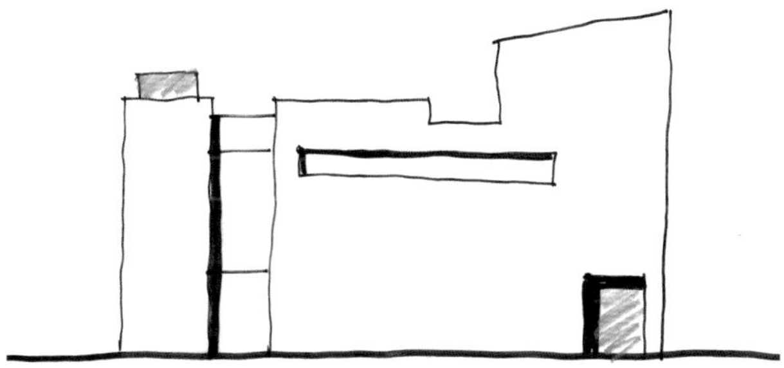

East A

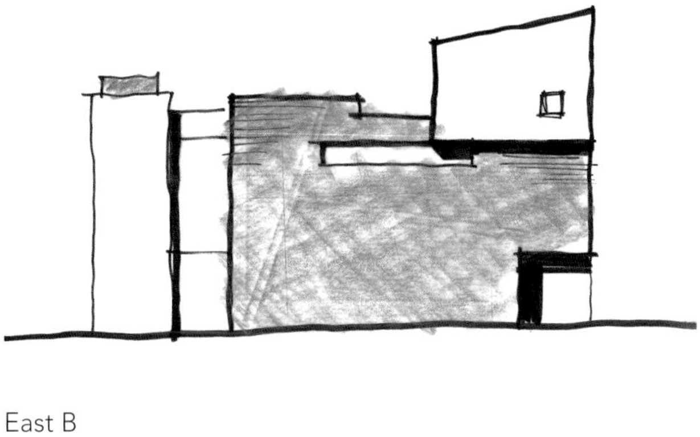

East B

North B

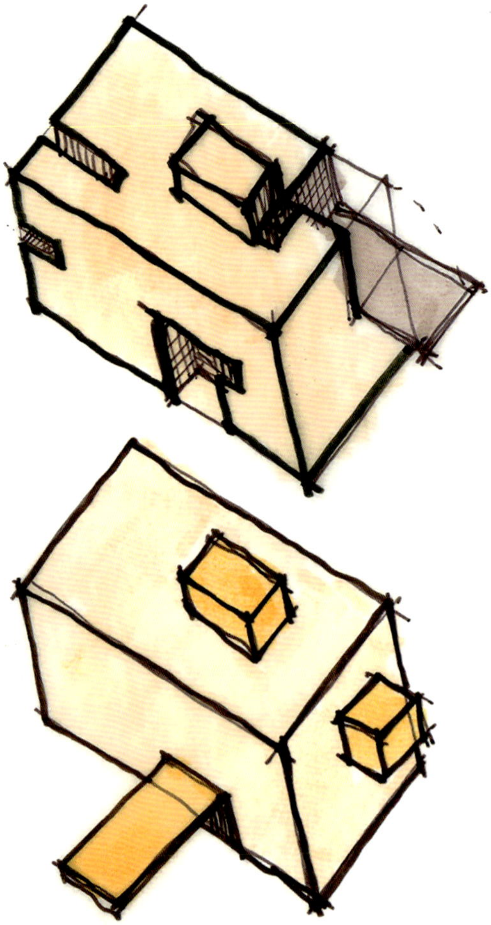

OPTION 4
1ST FLR

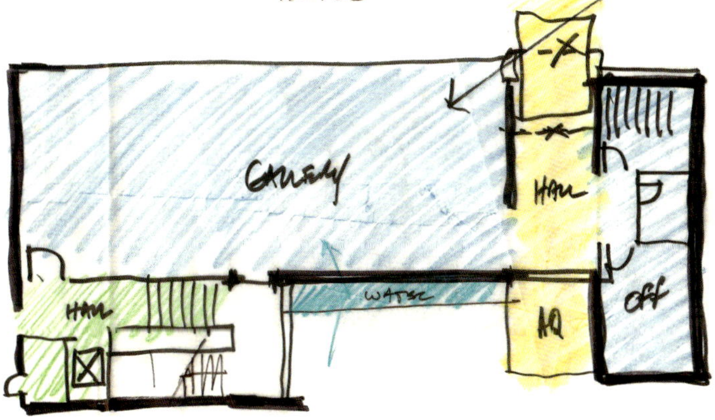

OPTION 4
2ND FLR

Presentation Drawings

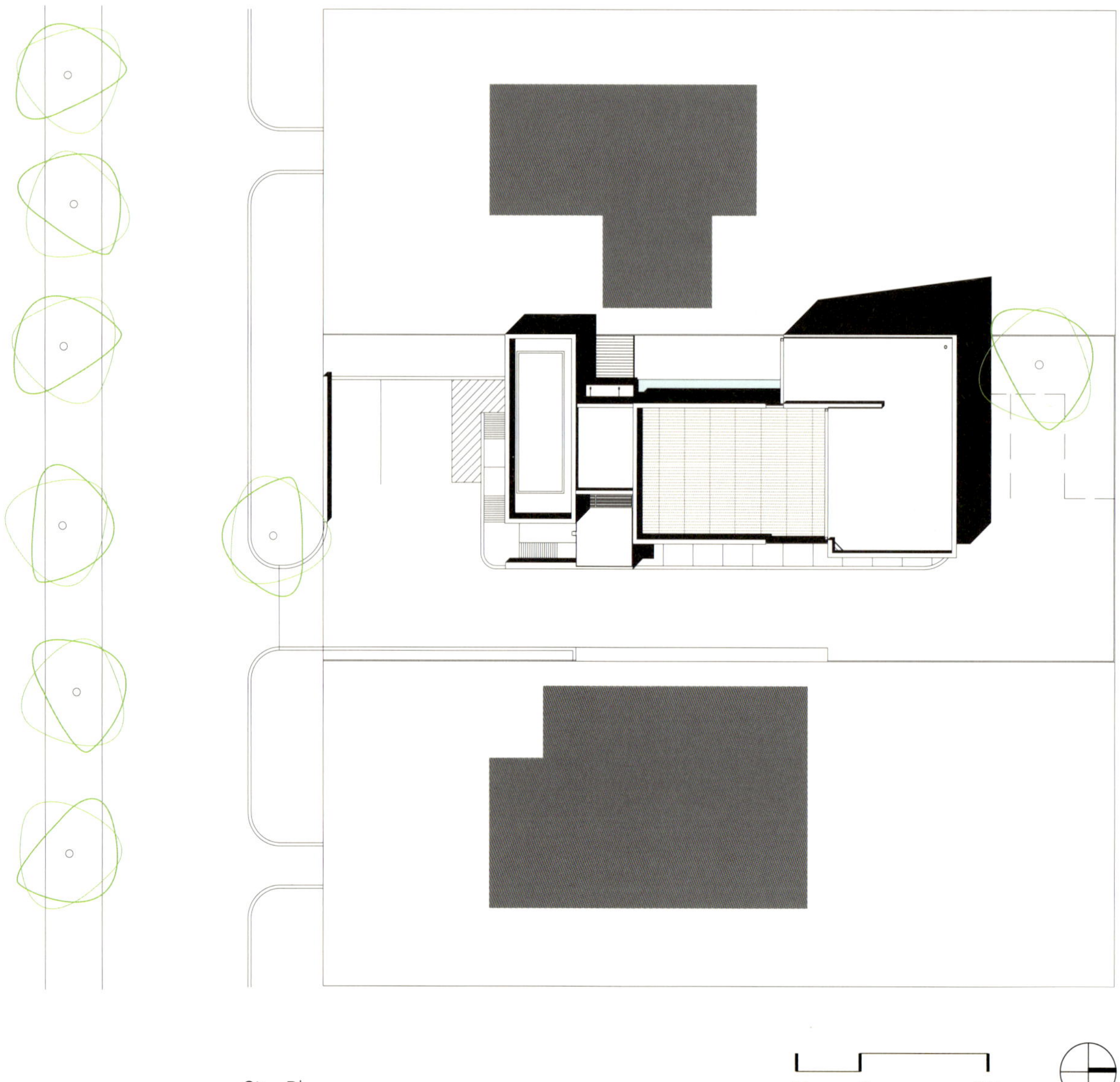

Site Plan

Third Floor

1 Restroom
2 Loft
3 Terrace

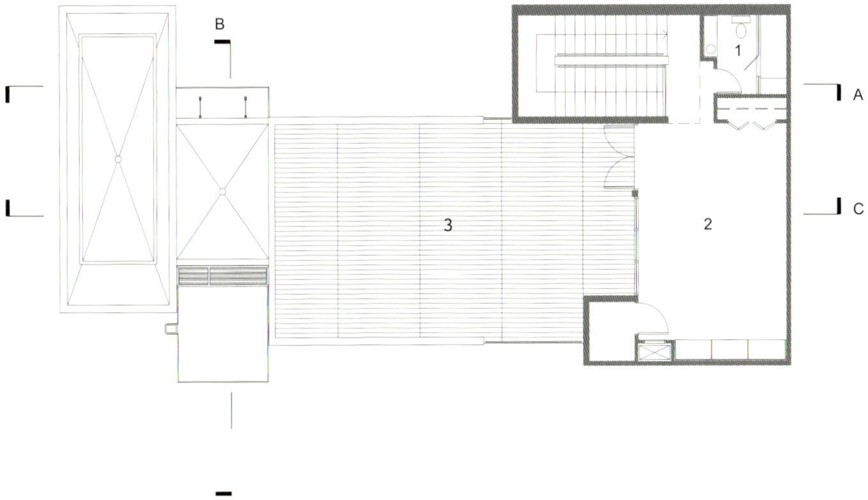

Second Floor

1 Storage
2 Gallery/Studio
3 Darkroom
4 Restroom

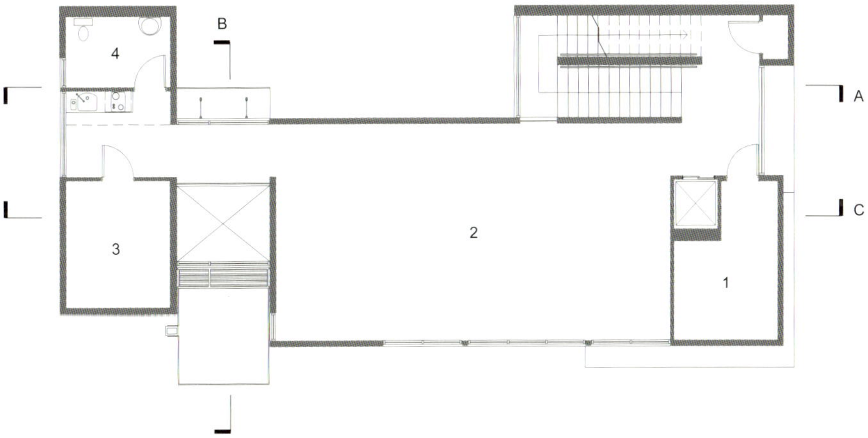

First Floor

1 Lobby
2 Office
3 Restroom
4 Gallery
5 Back entry
6 Sculpture garden

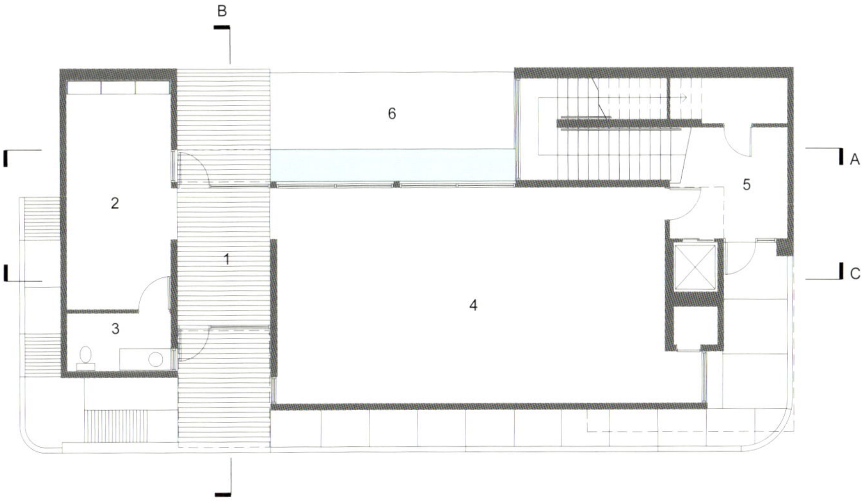

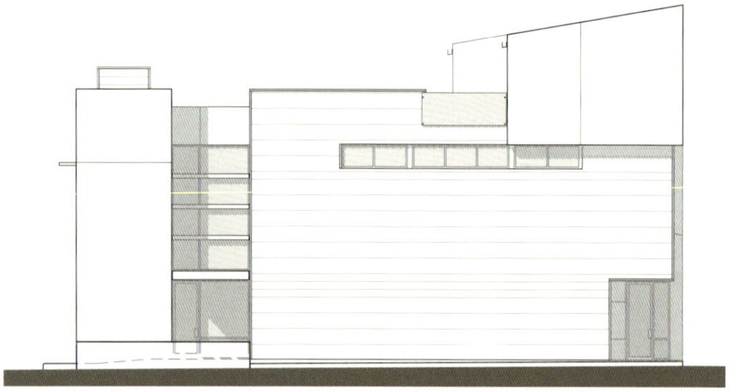

East Elevation

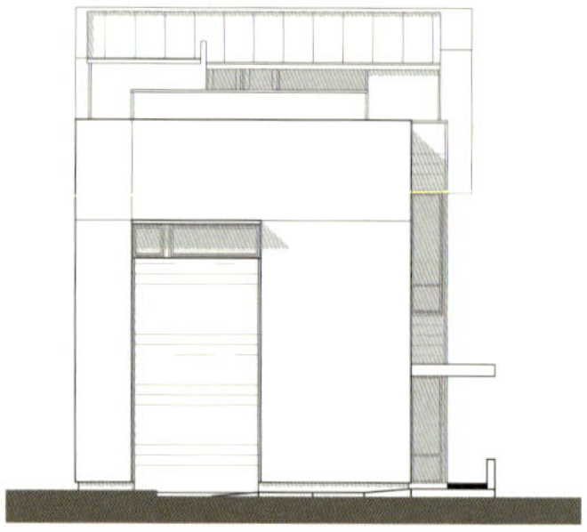

South Elevation

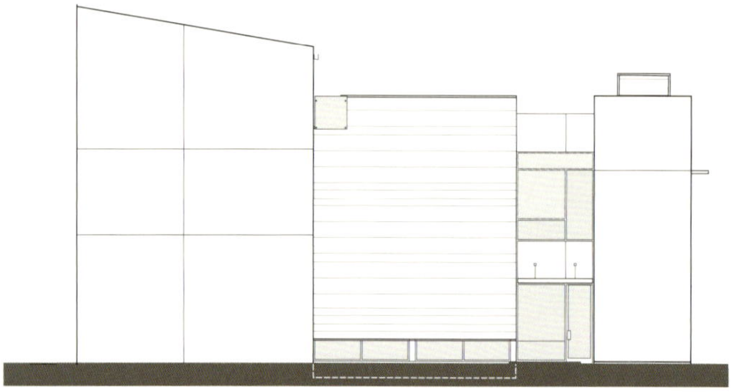

West Elevation

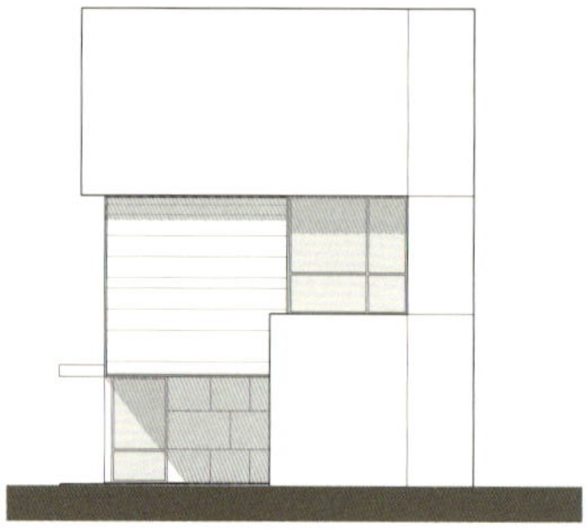

North Elevation

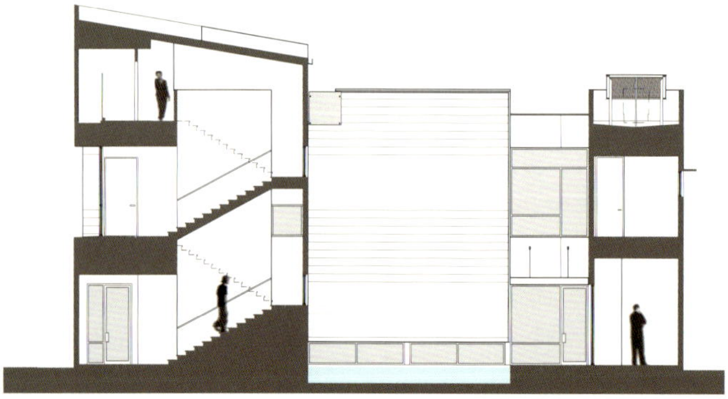

Section A

Section B

Axonometric

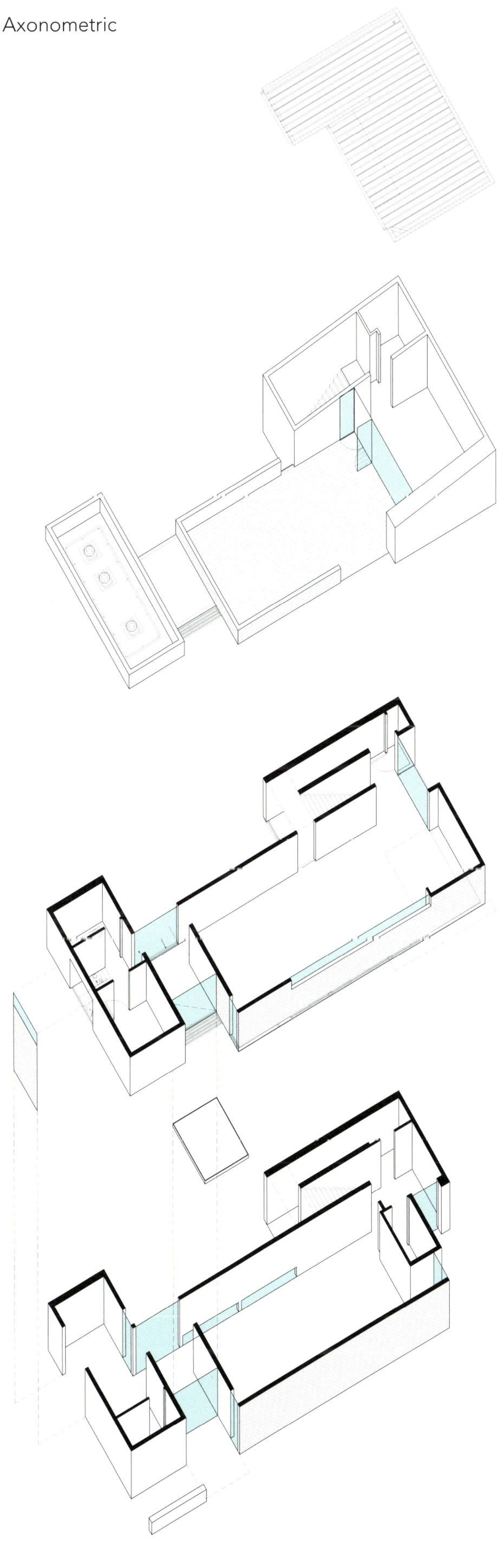

Renderings

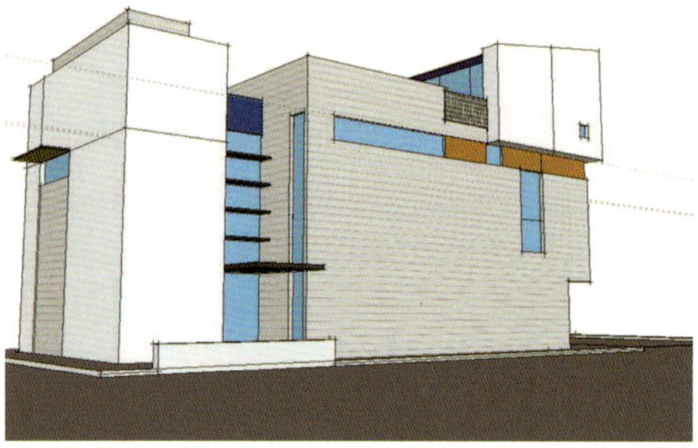

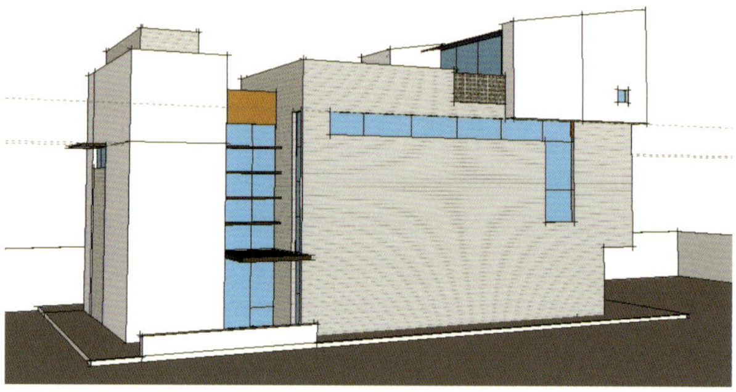

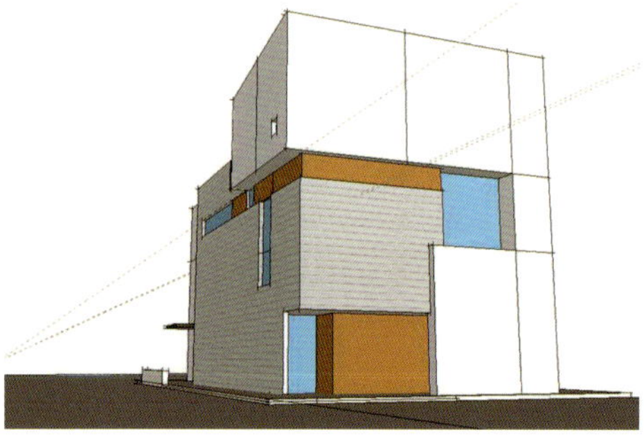

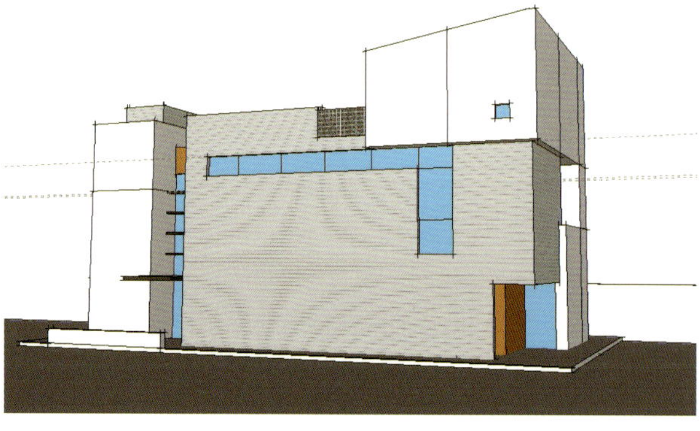

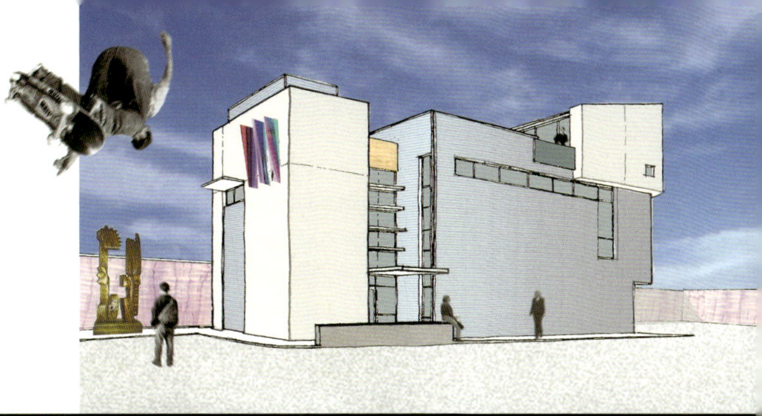

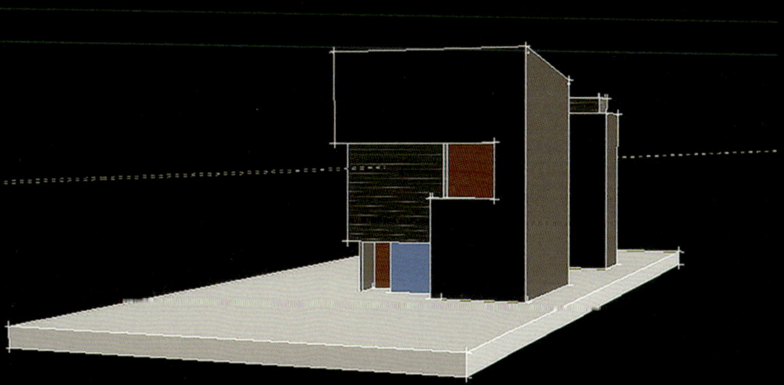

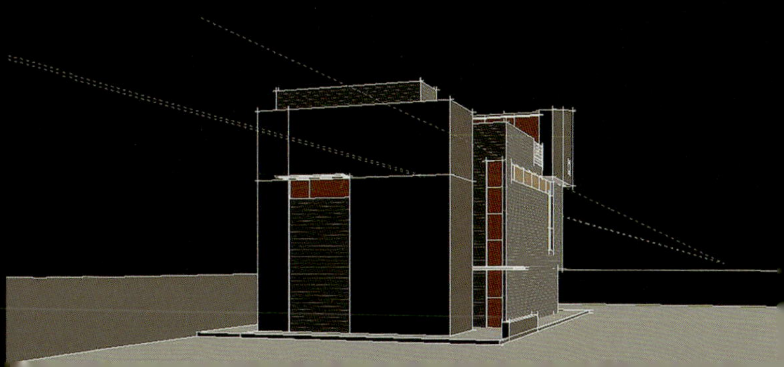

Diagrams

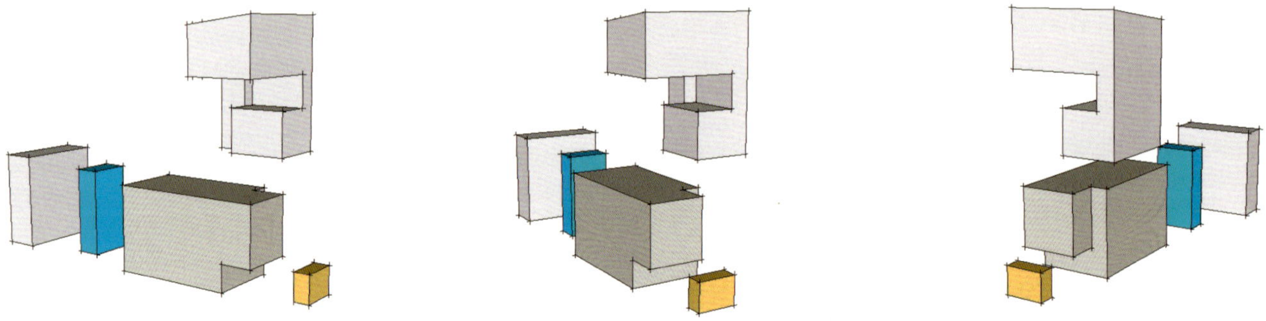

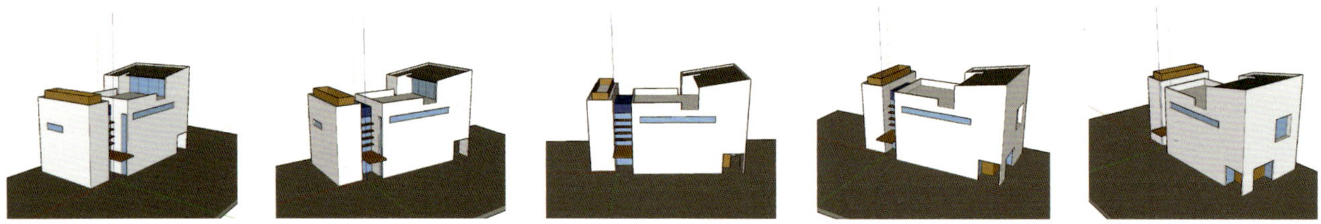

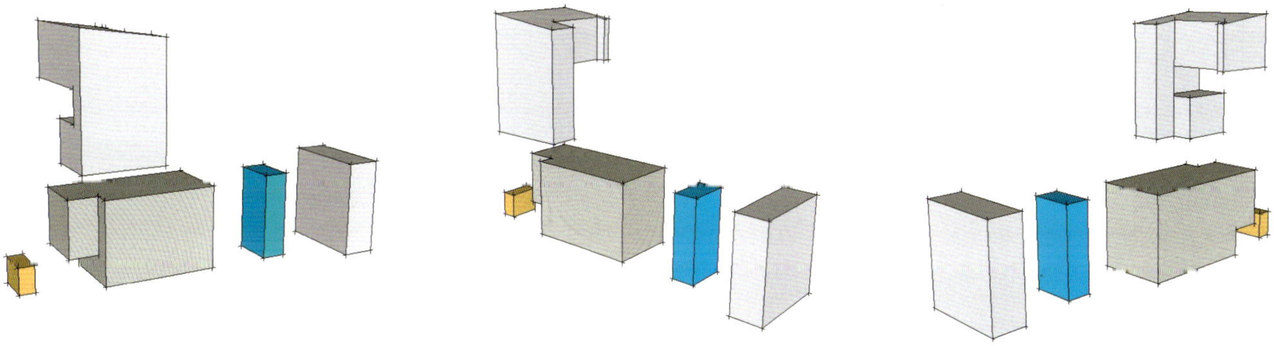

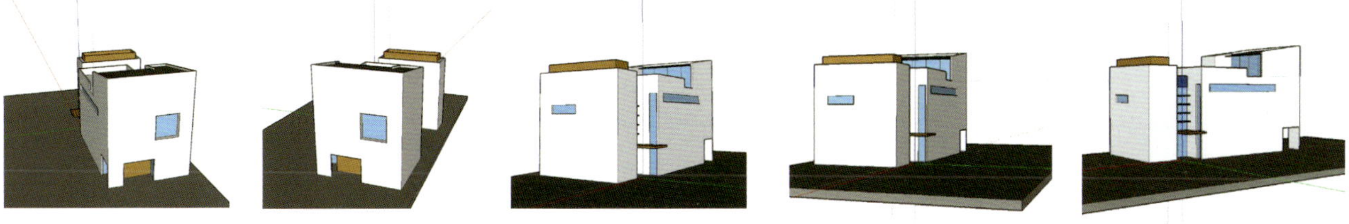

Models

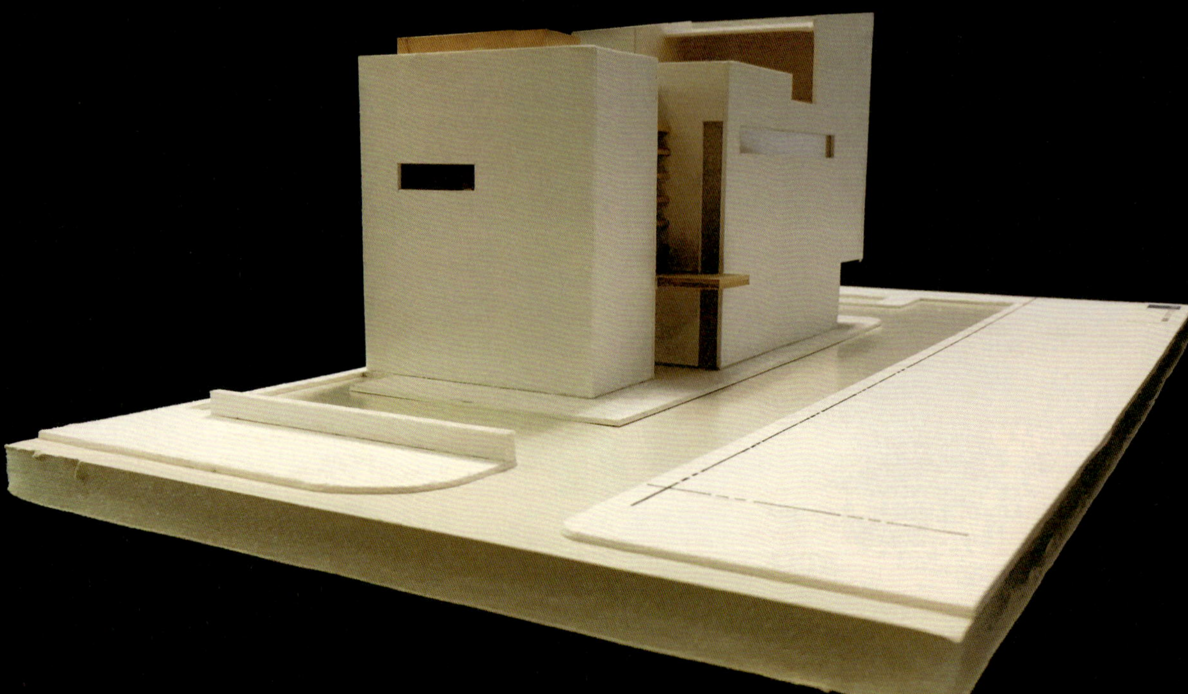

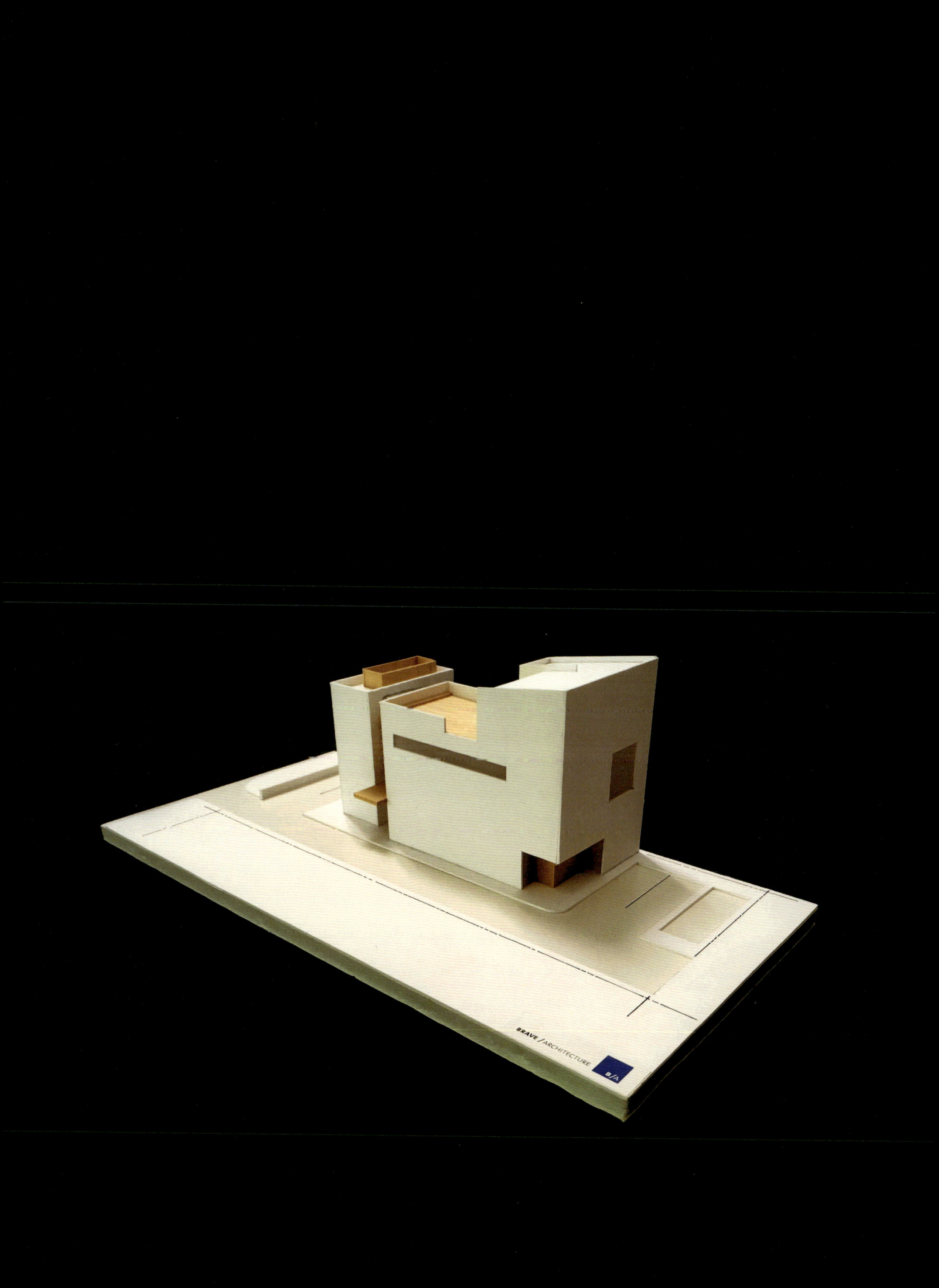
BRAVE / ARCHITECTURE
B/A

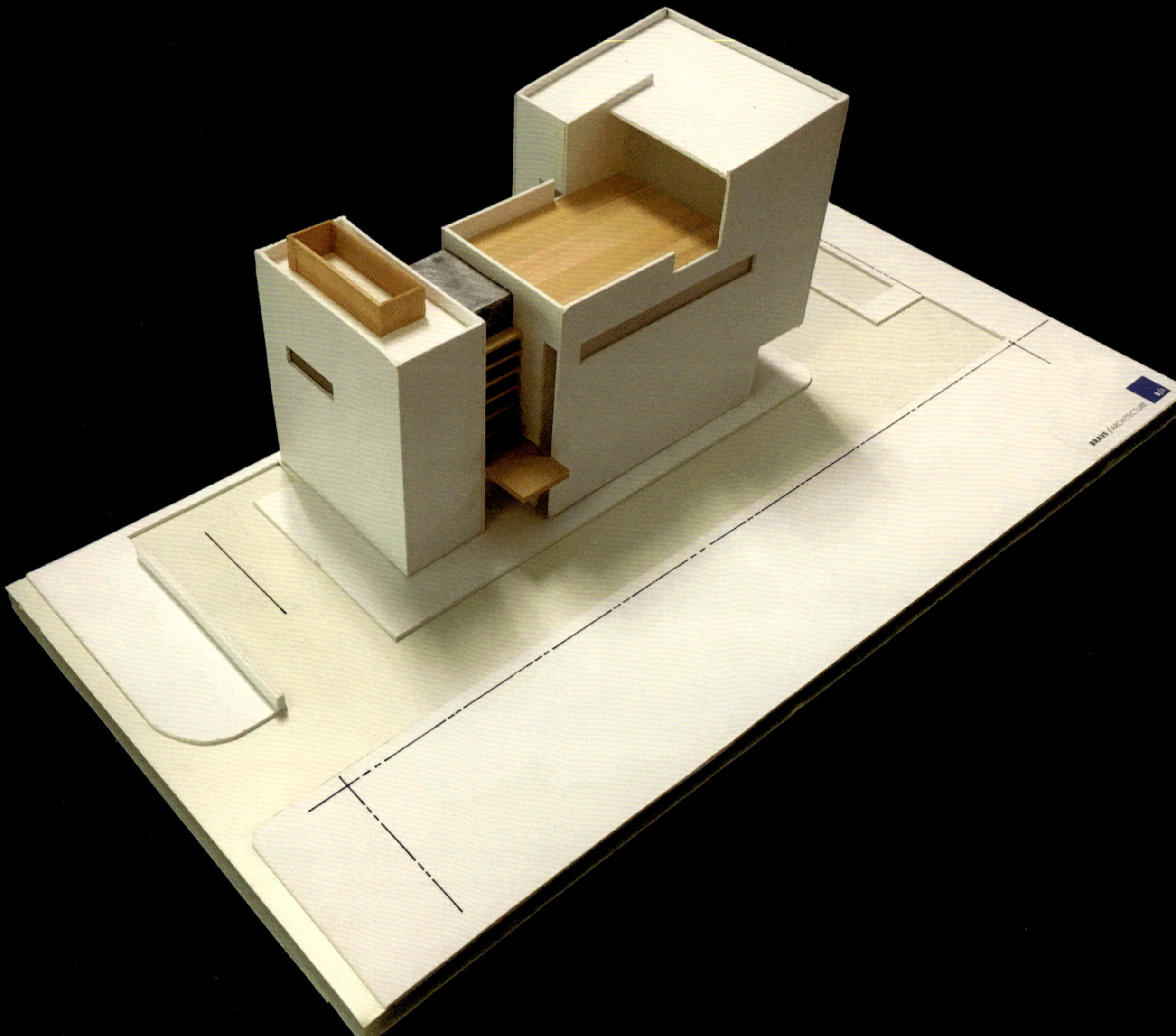

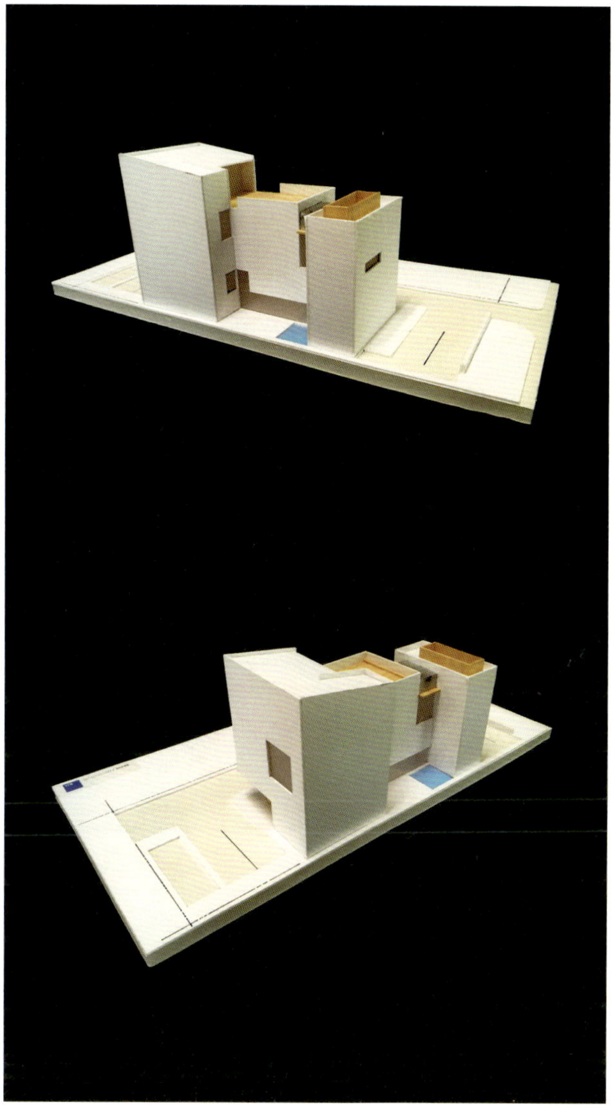

BRAVE / ARCHITECTURE
B/A

Construction

Tyvek
Tyvek
HomeWrap

Tyvek

Tyvek
HomeWrap

Tyvek
HomeWrap

The Building

De Santos Gallery

De Santos Gallery

ARCHITECTURE THROUGH
PHOTOGRAPHY: THREE VIEWS

ARCHITECTURE THROUGH
PHOTOGRAPHY: THREE VIEWS

ARCHITECTURE THROUGH
PHOTOGRAPHY: THREE VIEWS
CLAY HARMON PAUL HESTER VALENTIN L. GERTSMAN

Meet

VALENTIN L. GERTSMAN
CLAY HARMON

CHEMA MADOZ

PAUL HESTER

'Sicardi Gallery is so intriguing - it is the latest example of Houston's almost secret cohort of modern regional buildings' —— Ben Koush, AIA - Texas Architect 07 / 08 2014

Sicardi Gallery

Description

Located in the heart of Houston's Museum District, the Sicardi Gallery's design accommodates exhibitions of modern and contemporary work by Latin American artists living and working around the world. Most of the gallery's exhibits are large works, paintings, installations, objects, and video art. Established with the mission to facilitate a cultural dialogue between Latin America, the United States and Europe, Sicardi Gallery believes art to be a universal language and is a source of art and knowledge to museums around the world.

Placed adjacent to The Menil Collection's campus and across the street from the Houston Center for Photography, the project responds to the site's orientation and to its very specific neighboring qualities. The building's placement on a 50'x125' plot of land allows for maximum use of a small urban lot on a well-known urban corridor. The required width of the main gallery did not allow vehicle access to the back of the property, requiring the parking area to be in front of the building. The fortuitous result of this is that during opening nights, typically scheduled once a month, the front parking area is turned into an impromptu exterior social gathering place. The building exterior is cladded in large-rib, enameled, galvanized steel panels and white cement stucco.

Much like the De Santos Gallery, located a half mile away, the massing of the Sicardi Gallery is the result of a formulaic application of the project's space program as well as the many site-specific constraints, including a high-voltage power line at the back of the property. The building's program is organized on both floors along a linear circulation spine. Wider, larger spaces requiring less natural light are placed on the west side of the building, while offices and spaces benefiting from ambient natural light are placed along the east side. The building's two main galleries, one on each floor, receive indirect natural light that can be controlled where necessary for specific art installations and to enhance the visitors' experience.

The building's interiors are finished in drywall over a special substrate allowing the easy installation and removal of art while requiring minimum maintenance. The ground floor is sealed concrete while the upper level's is tongue-and-groove southern yellow pine planks. The building's lighting system is composed of continuous, linear T-5 light tubes.

Additional exhibit spaces are sprinkled throughout the building along the main circulation spine. Display and work spaces are interconnected providing clear circulation, but allowing for privacy where needed. The main exhibit areas on the ground floor have 16' high ceilings. Additionally, the ground floor accommodates the reception, administrative offices, storage space, a workroom, kitchenette, and other support spaces.

Next to the second level's gallery there is a large storage and display area, affectionately called the "back-room". Executive offices and a research library are also placed on this level. An outdoor terrace for displaying sculptures serves as a decompression feature during large gatherings. Conceived as a stand-alone, compositional element in plan and volume, the stair doubles as a social gathering space and offers through a 10'x12' window a unique view of Alabama Avenue's mature oak trees that dress the Menil's campus across the street.

Recently renamed Sicardi Ayers Bacino, the gallery is one of the cultural building blocks enhancing the artistic fabric of Houston's Museum District.

Project Data

Project Size
5,400 SF

Lot Size
50′ x 125′

Project Location
Houston, Texas

Completed
2012

Architect
BRAVE / ARCHITECTURE

Project Team
Fernando L. Brave, FAIA
Alp Bozkurt
Bryant Alcantara
Alejandro Brave

Consultants
Matrix Structural Engineers
Structural

TGK & Associates
MEP

General Contractor
Arch-Con Corporation

Design Awards
Community Improvement Award - Museum District Business Alliance, 2012

Design Award - AIA Houston, 2015

A Tin Gallery by Ben Koush

The Houston architectural scene has long been something of an anomaly, compared with the rest of the state. Unlike such well-known "Texas" architects as O'Neil Ford, FAIA; Frank Welch, FAIA; Ted Flato, FAIA; and David Lake, FAIA, Houston's modern architects have not been preoccupied with creating a regional building culture. In fact, during a symposium at The University of Texas at Austin School of Architecture in 1981, Howard Barnstone, FAIA, Houston's best-known modern architect, casually compared regionalism to candy, or dope: "It gives you a big lift, then lets you down." (TA Nov./Dec., 1981) Fellow panel members Ford, Welch, and Larry Speck, FAIA, weren't pleased.

This is one big reason why Brave/Architecture's recently completed building for the Sicardi Gallery is so intriguing. It is the latest example of Houston's almost secret cohort of modern regional buildings, which Barnstone himself paradoxically instigated in the late 1960s. In retrospect, what Barnstone might have been criticizing was not the idea of an architecture tied to a place, but rather a sentimental and simplistic regionalism that in its Texas iteration substitutes limestone, rough-hewn beams, and lone stars for a critical engagement with the conditions of modernity.

In 1969, along with his then-business partner Eugene Aubry, FAIA, Barnstone designed a building on the Rice University campus for John and Dominique de Menil's newly created Institute of the Arts. Both the exterior walls and gable roof of the 60-ft-by-200-ft warehouse-like building were clad in sheets of cheap corrugated galvanized iron, commonly used on light industrial buildings in Houston at the time. The Art Barn, as it was affectionately known, was an unlikely oasis of culture for nearly 20 years. And yet, despite its long life, its popularity, and vigorous protests, the Art Barn was demolished by Rice in April 2014. By appropriating the ordinary materials and forms of Houston's generic metal warehouses and then asserting the result as "architecture," Barnstone and Aubry produced a subversive art building in the same postwar pop spirit that gave rise to Andy Warhol's soup cans and Roy Lichtenstein's comic strips. True to this spirit, the Menils exhibited works from their art collection in the Art Barn until they decamped in 1987 to a permanent museum building.

Once the Art Barn was in operation, these sorts of buildings — simple masses clad entirely in corrugated metal — began to multiply. Built mostly by members of the art community in marginal neighborhoods, where deed restrictions had either never existed or long since lapsed, these "Tin Houses" slowly became recognized as an architectural phenomenon by the 1990s. Fernando Brave, FAIA, was part of the wave. In 1994, he designed and built a Tin House for his family in Houston's West End, the epicenter of the movement.

Essay published in Texas Architecture,
TSA Design Awards, Issue Number 64/04,
September/October 2005
www.texasarchitect.org

That same year, after relocating from Buenos Aires to Houston, María Inés Sicardi opened her eponymous gallery to display Latin American avant-garde art. She began by operating out of a 700-sf space in a small Montrose office complex on Kipling Street where she was able to show prints and small paintings, but not much else. In 2001, a move next door to the McClain Gallery building on Richmond Avenue, a 1,700-sf space with 14-ft-tall ceilings, allowed Sicardi to show more spatially demanding works by such artists as Gego (Gertrud Goldschmidt), Carlos Cruz-Diez, and Jesús Rafael Soto. Her appetite whetted for presenting still larger works — and prompted by a fear of disruptive Metro light-rail construction — Sicardi prepared to move again. Brave designed her current gallery space, which was completed in 2012.

According to Brave, a fellow transplant from Argentina, as Sicardi searched for a suitable site along local thoroughfares, she kept coming back to West Alabama Street. She was attracted by its manageable traffic and proximity to the Menil Collection. The property she ultimately acquired is directly across from the museum's parking lot, and she worked out an arrangement with the Menil Collection to allow visitors to park there during art openings.

Sicardi's design requirements were almost entirely based on accommodating artworks that were too large for the gallery space on Richmond Avenue. The new building contains 5,900 sf divided into two floors. Ceilings on the first floor are 16-ft-tall, and they reach 12 ft on the second level. "She's built a little museum," said Brave, looking around the big first-floor gallery. The rest of the building mass was determined by code setbacks and easements, which are responsible for its boxy, carved-away final shape. The exterior of the building is almost entirely clad in large-scale, silver-colored corrugated galvalume panels. The entrance is stucco painted white, and the fire-rated walls along the western property line are made of exposed concrete block. At the front elevation, a 24-ft-tall metal-wrapped volume, pierced by a single 12-ft-by-12-ft window, hovers serenely over a recessed 10-ft-tall lower section, which houses the main entrance doors. Although this arrangement seems to deliberately invert the actual interior division of the building, Brave explained that this was done on purpose to provide an entry scaled to people rather than to the art. The asymmetrical grid pattern of dark grey gravel embedded in the concrete paving at the front of the building will ultimately be continued to the property next door, where architect Dillon Kyle, AIA, is planning a new building for his practice.

Inside, the spaces are standard-issue art gallery. Walls are painted a uniform bright white. There is exposed, light grey concrete on the first floor and natural finished pine on the second floor. Lighting is deliberately crude. Linear fluorescent light fixtures in Dan Flavin-like, single-file lines are supplemented in a few places by track lights. The cool, uniform light they produce is currently popular in the art world. Sicardi had seen such arrangements in galleries in Rio de Janeiro and Paris before selecting it for hers. Despite the avant-garde appeal of this system, the generous and lofty galleries seem to deserve better.

The new "Tin" Sicardi Gallery building strongly suggests that the now 45-year-old Tin Building movement remains viable in Houston. Its elegantly resolved design and level of craftsmanship indicate a refinement of the cheeky bravado of its inaugural buildings. However, whereas the first Tin Buildings resonated because they brought Houston's industrial vernacular into the language of art, the Sicardi Gallery's carefully composed, neo-modern elevations and graceful proportions begin to seem conservative. Drawing from the established architectural imagery of the International Style instead of from "non-buildings" with no style, this new building does not quite replicate the dialectical act that made the first Tin Buildings so captivating.

In 1994, Drexel Turner, who was the first to analyze the Tin Buildings as an architectural trend peculiar to Houston, wrote: "For all its virtues, latent and apparent, sheet metal — particularly in its shiny, corrugated form — has become something of an architectural comfort food, no longer shocking enough to antagonize the bourgeoisie but still vestigially progressive enough to signal intention and perhaps even deflect closer scrutiny." Although almost 20 years have passed since his observations were published in Cite magazine, they still ring true. They suggest the difficulty of creating relevant architecture of place and bring to mind some questions: What scrutiny is being deflected? How can a regionally-inflected architecture stay one step ahead of the deadening effects of modern culture? Would it have been possible for this building to be as progressive as the art it contains? How far can the architectural language of a contemporary art gallery be pushed?

Ben Koush is an architect in Houston.

Sketches

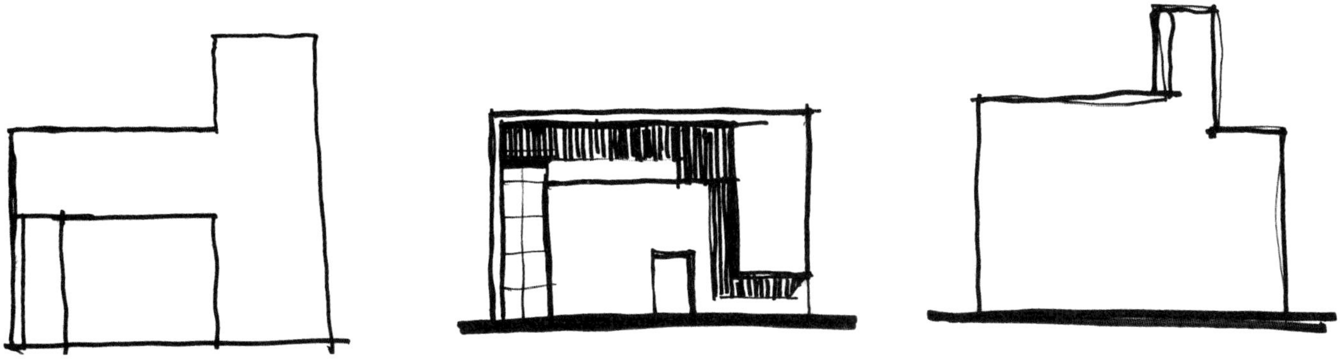

Front

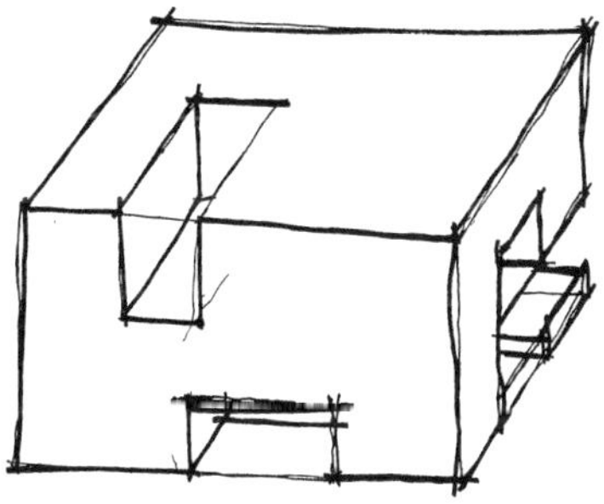

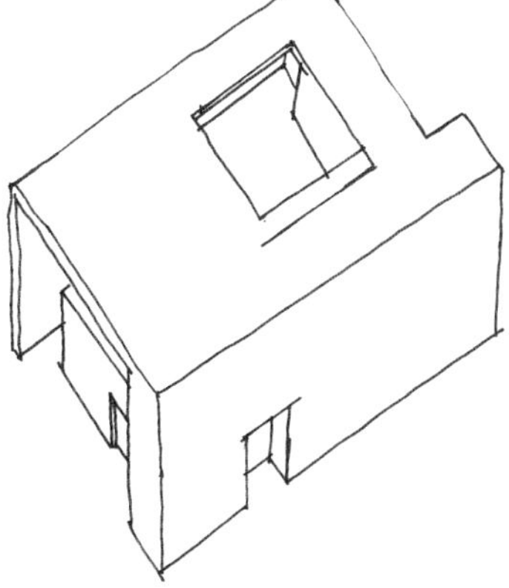

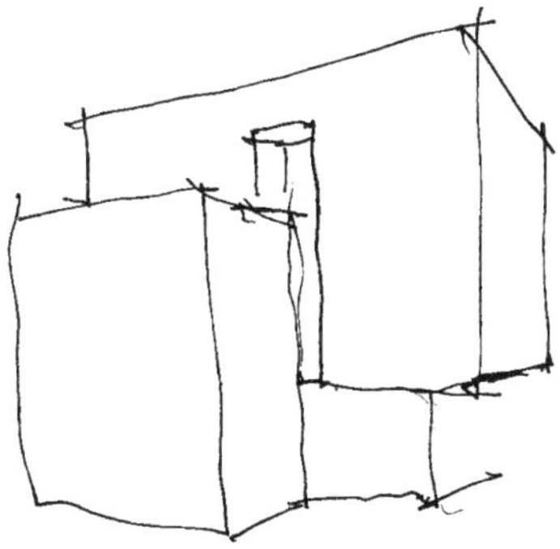

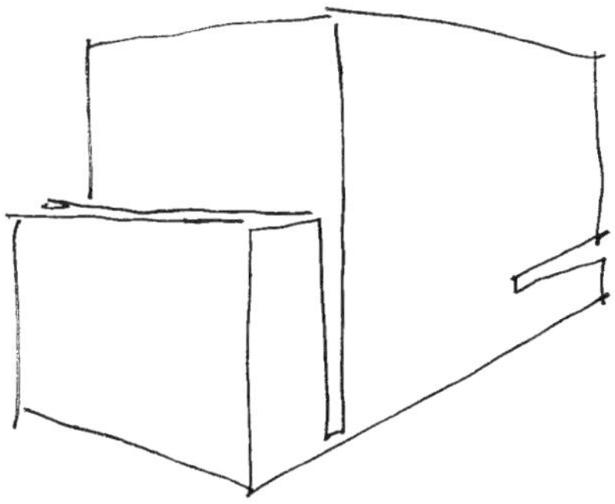

GLASS

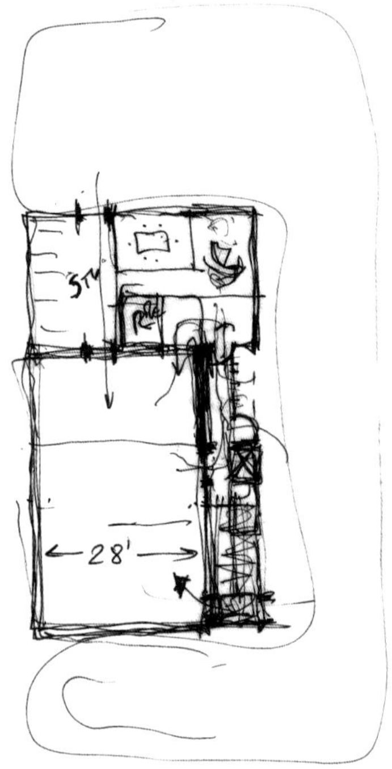
STG
28'

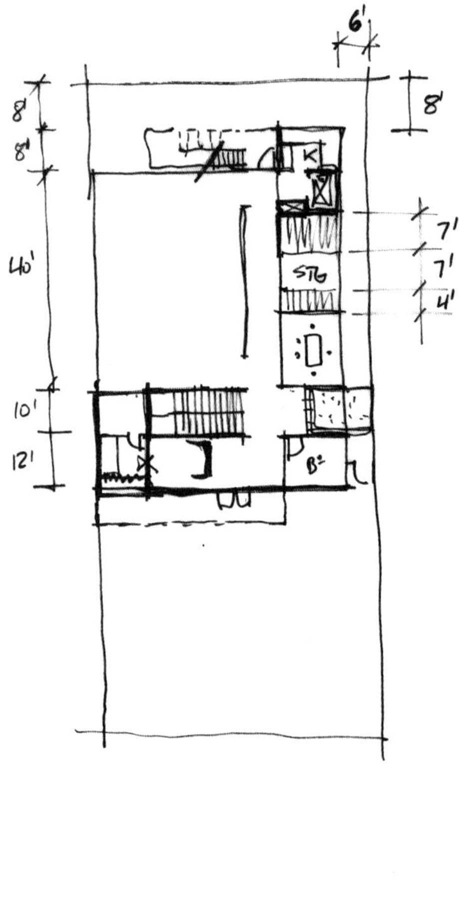
6'
8'
8'
8'
40'
7'
7'
4'
STG
K
10'
12'
B²

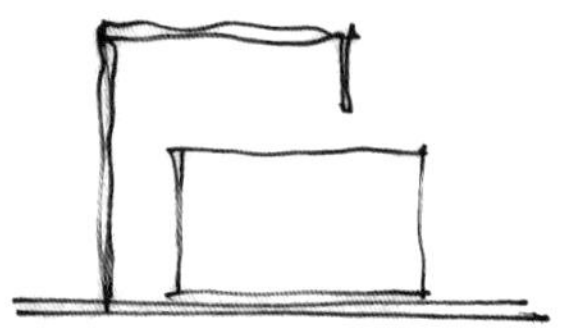

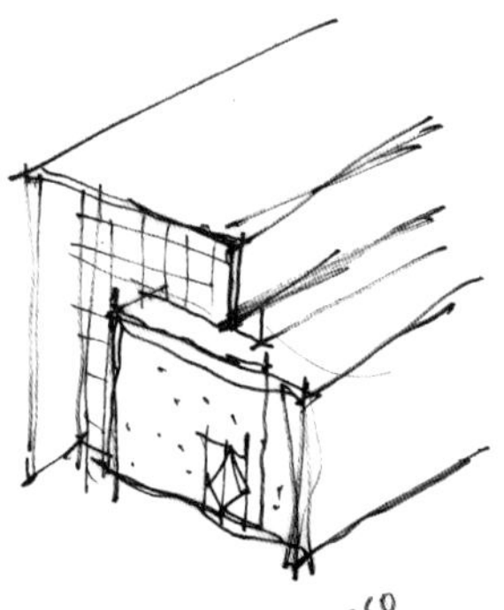

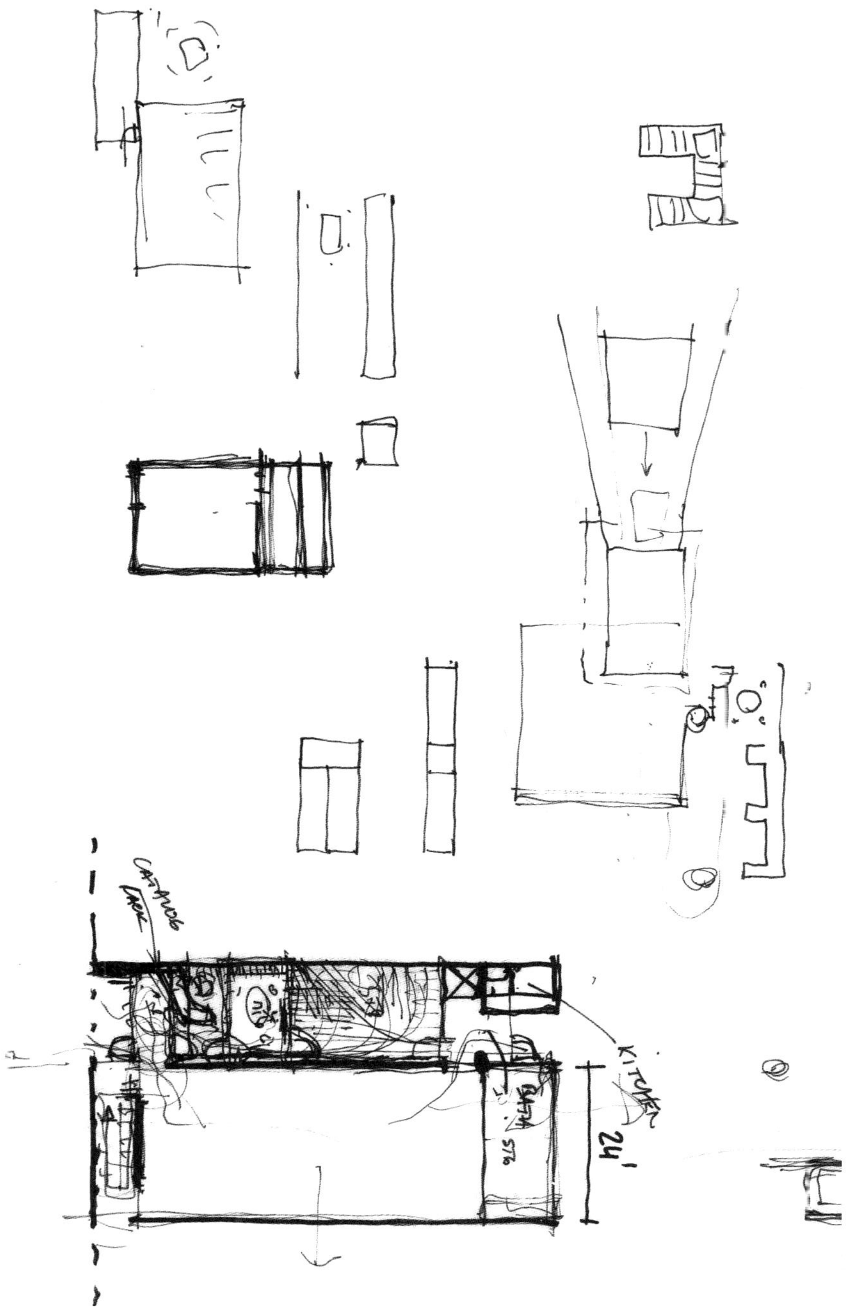
KITCHEN
24'
BATH

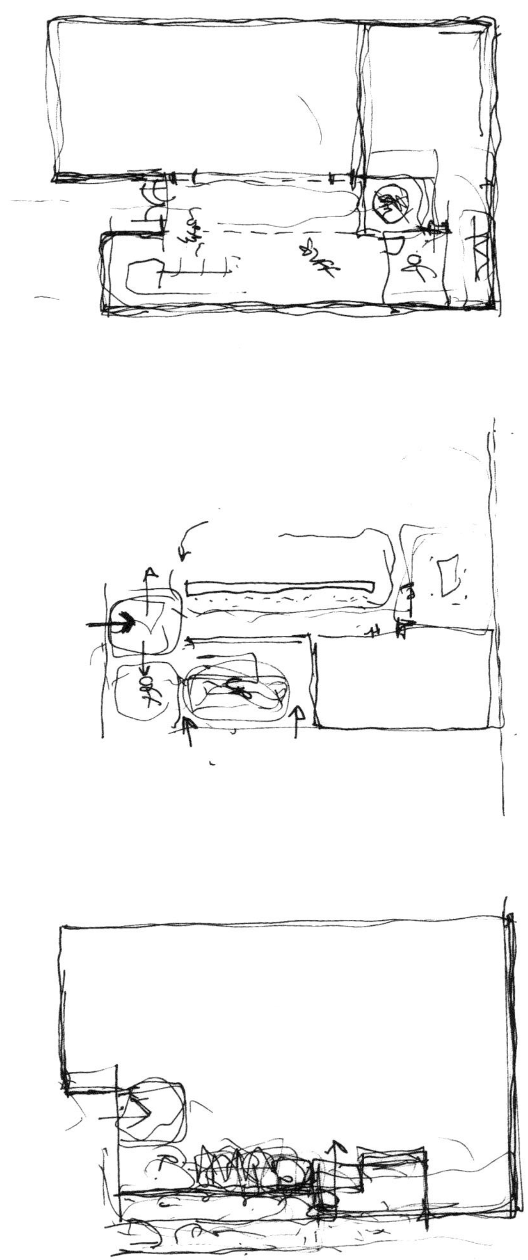

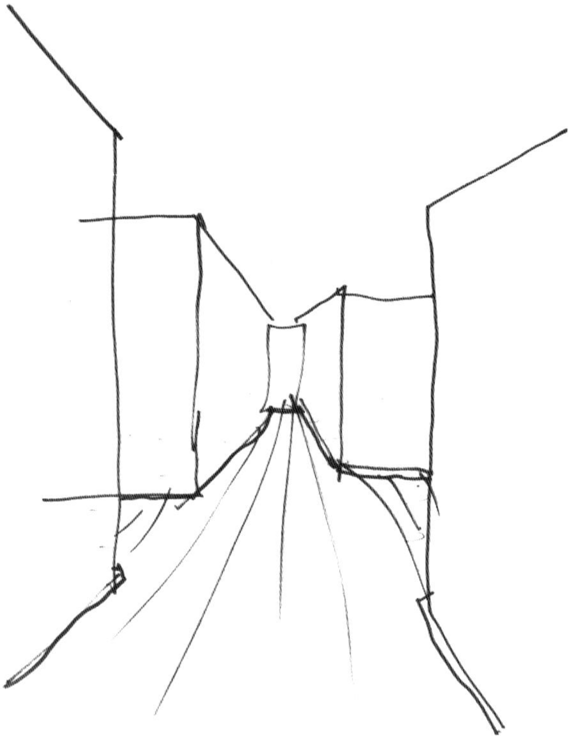

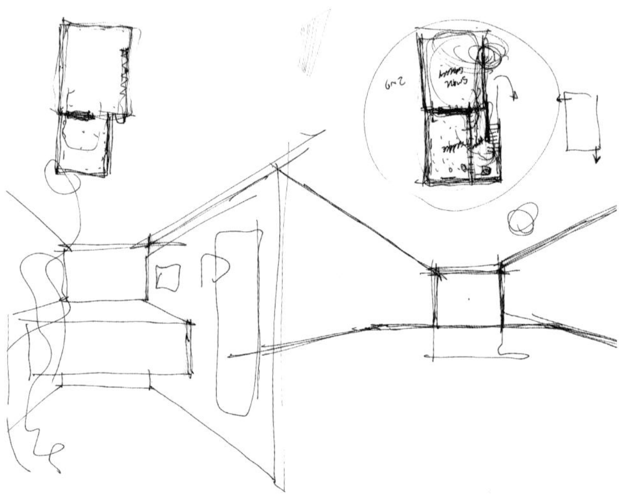

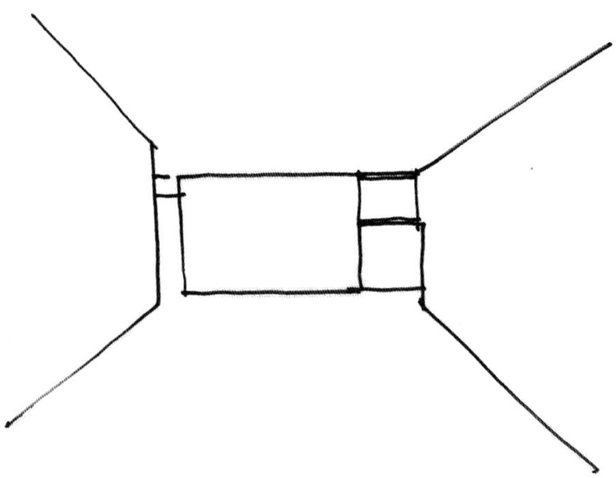

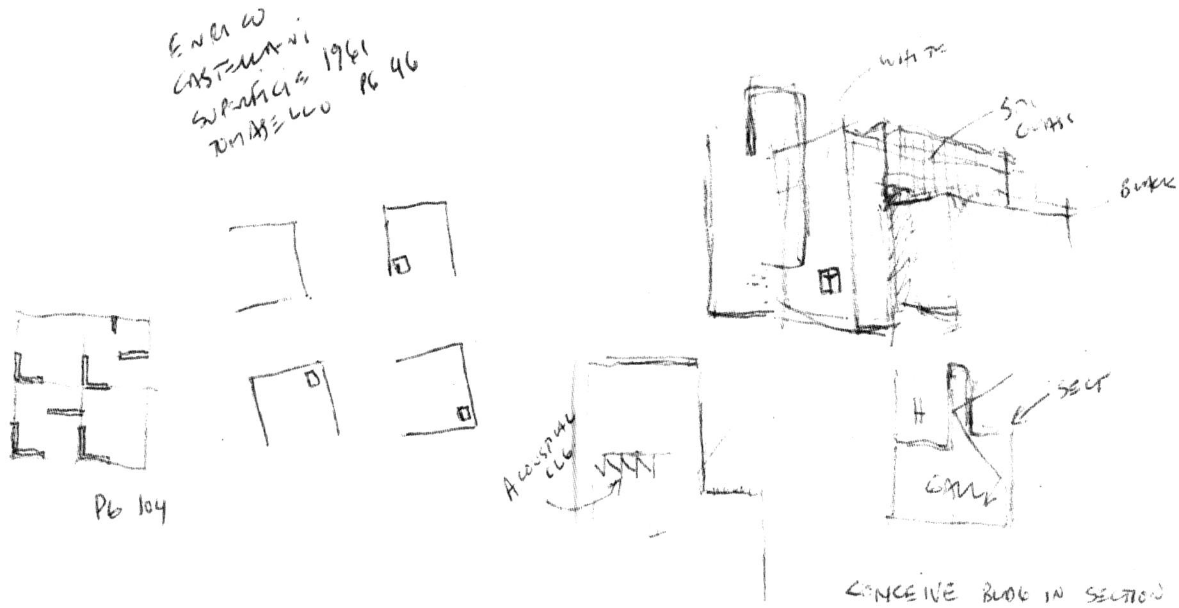
PG 104
BLACK
SECT
CONCEIVE BLDG IN SECTION

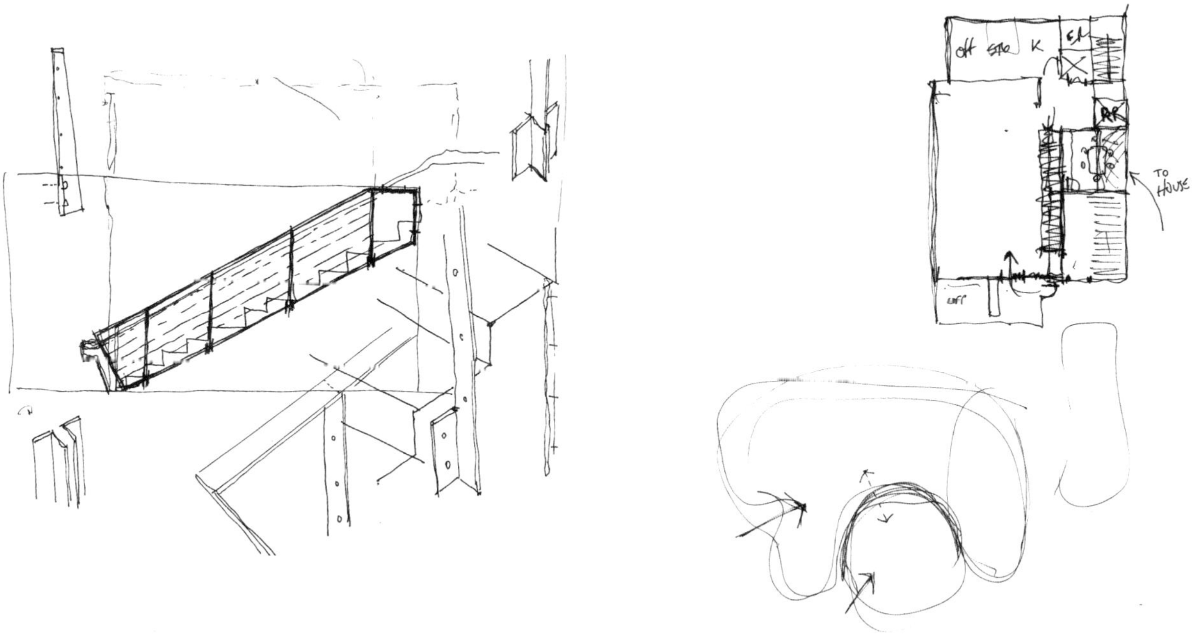
TO HOUSE

Presentation Drawings

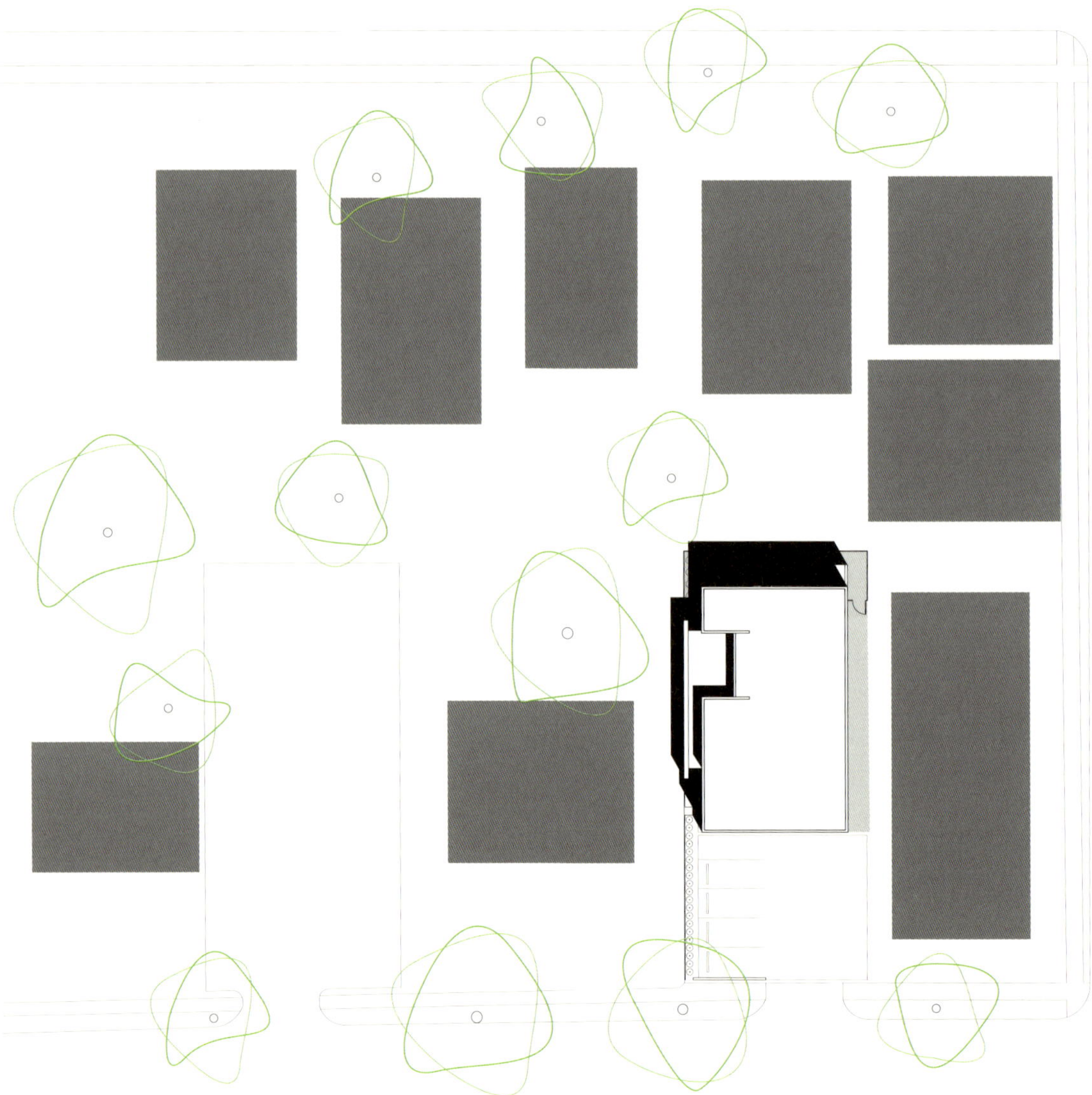

Site Plan

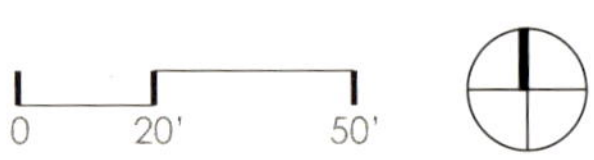

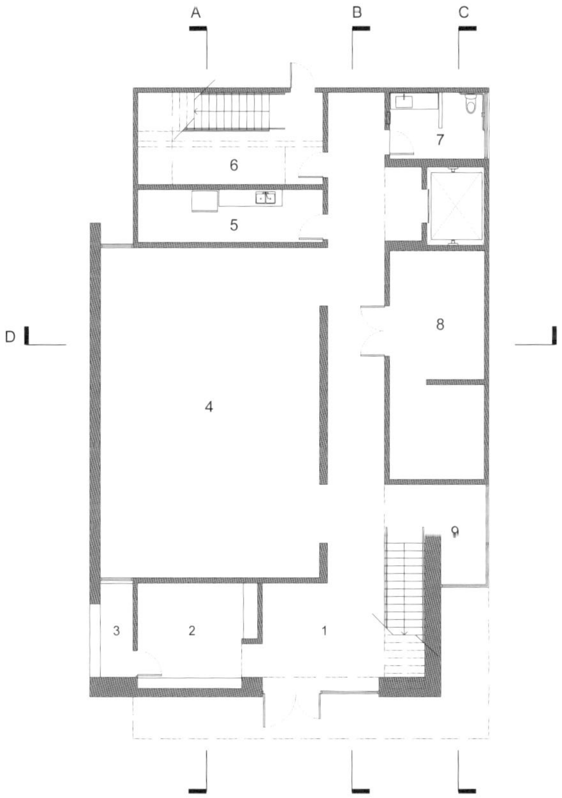

First Floor

1 Lobby
2 Office
3 Patio
4 Large gallery
5 Kitchenette
6 Storage
7 Restroom
8 Work room
9 Art niche

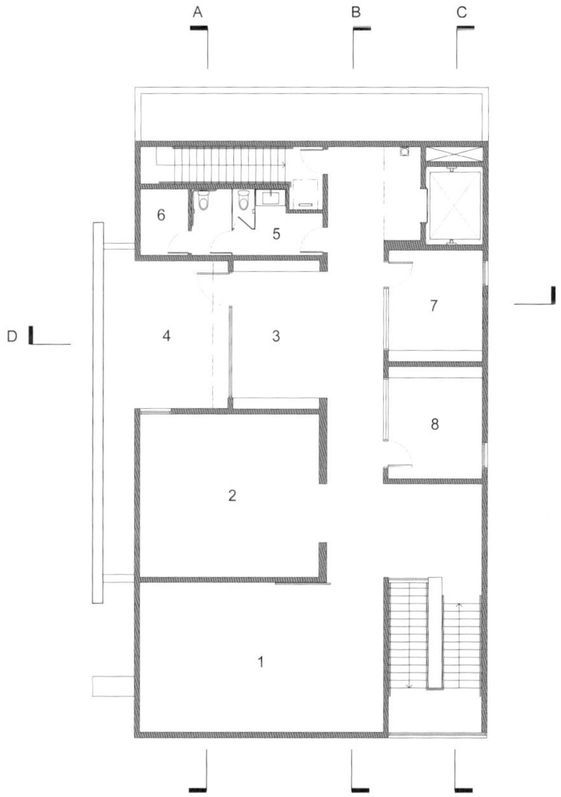

Second Floor

1 Art storage
2 Small gallery
3 Library
4 Sculpture terrace
5 Rest room
6 Mechanical
7 Office
8 Office

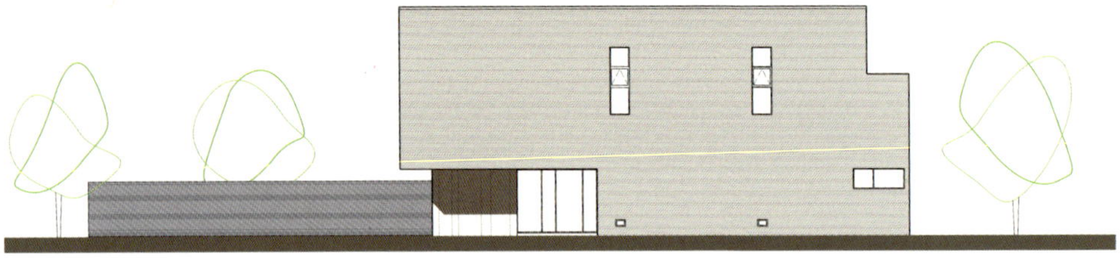

East Elevation

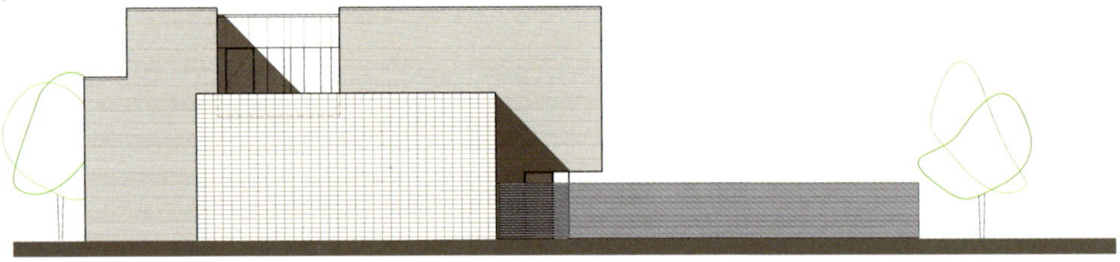

West Elevation

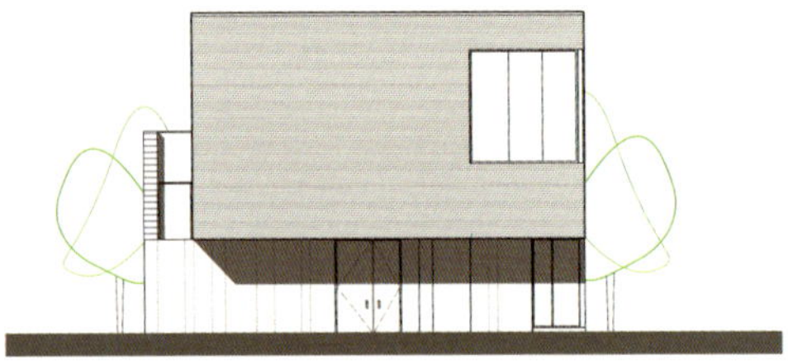

South Elevation

Section A

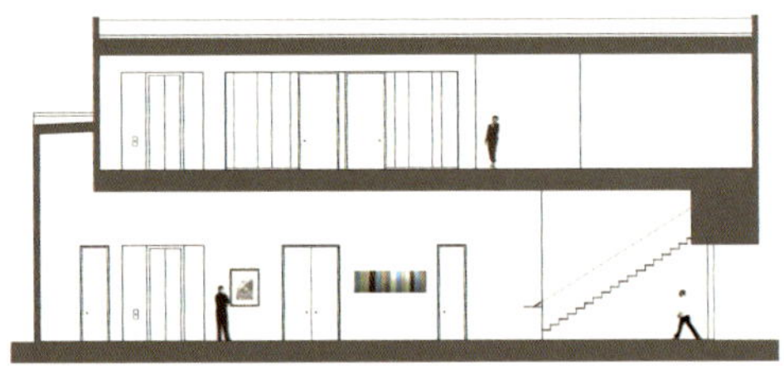

Section B

Section C

Section D

Axonometric

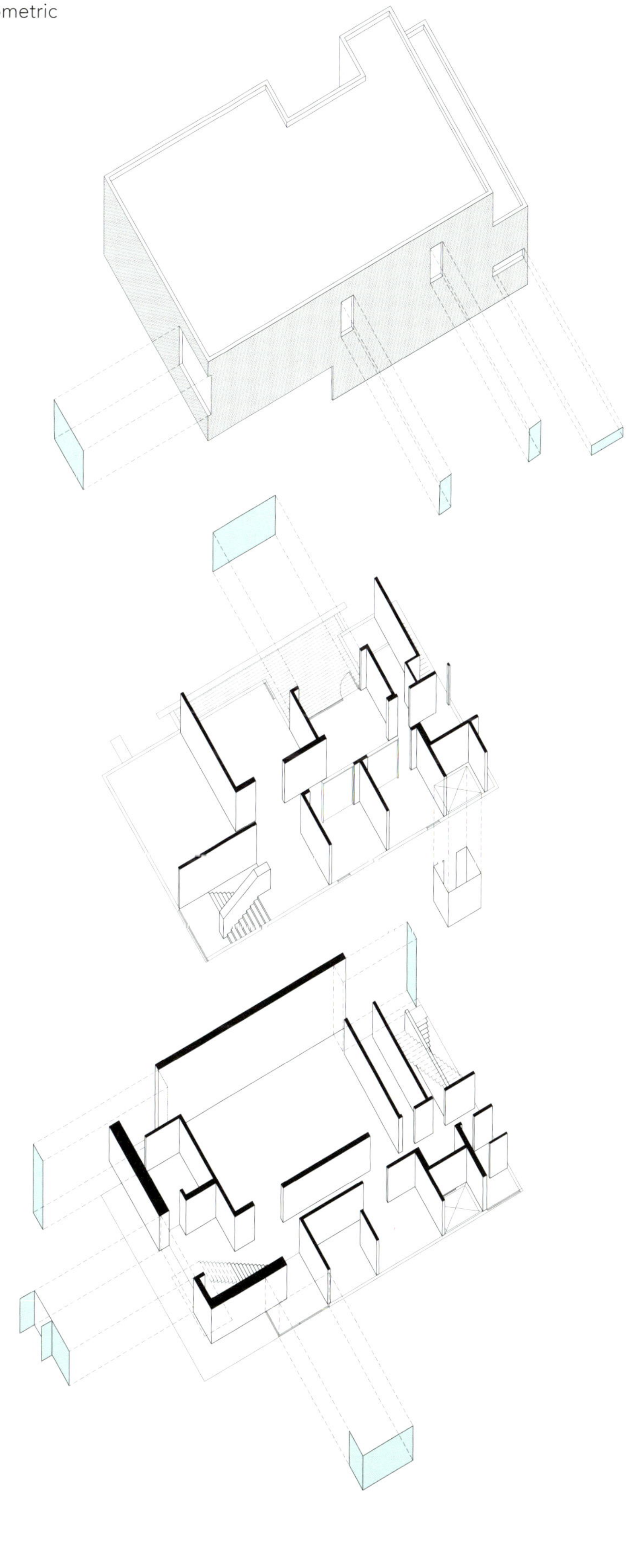

Renderings

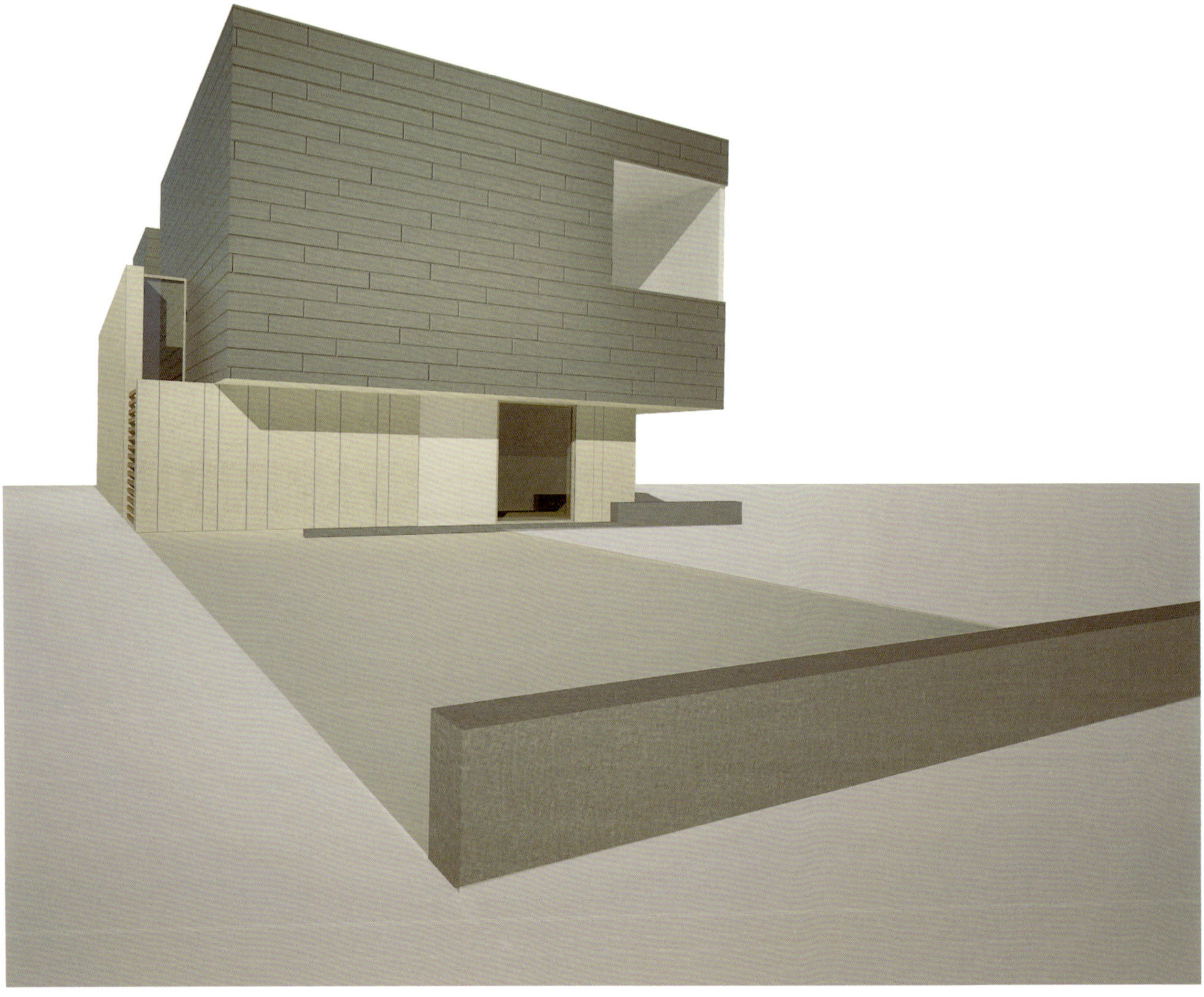

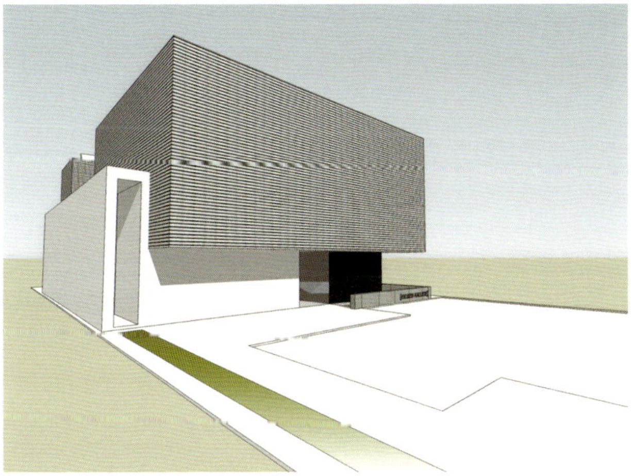

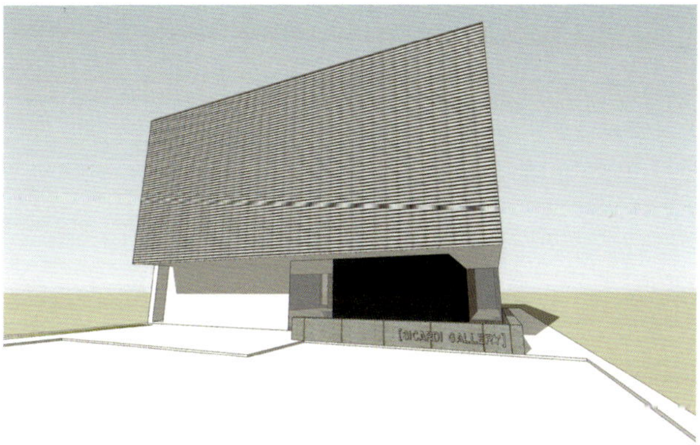
[SICARDI GALLERY]

Diagrams

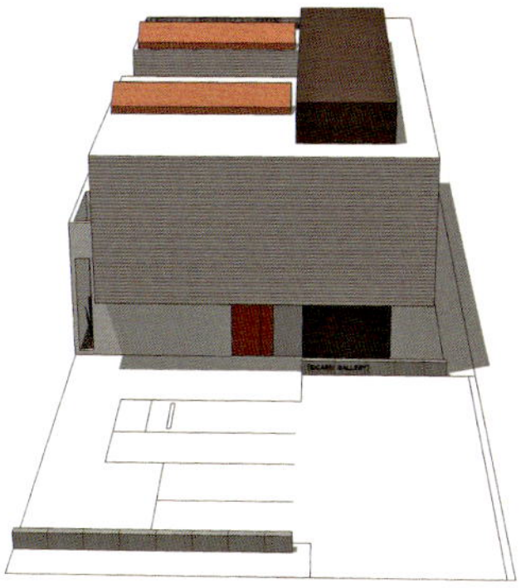

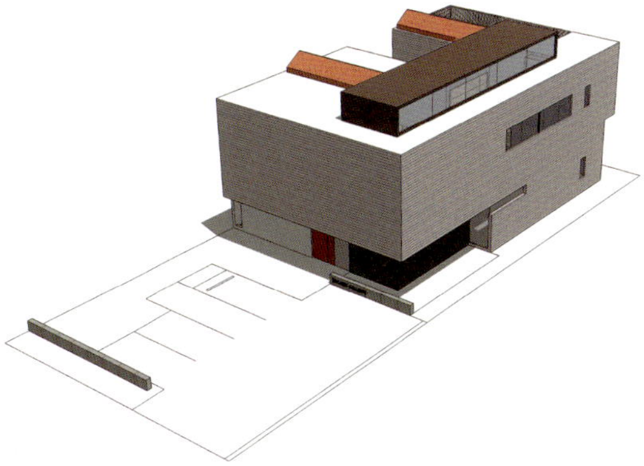

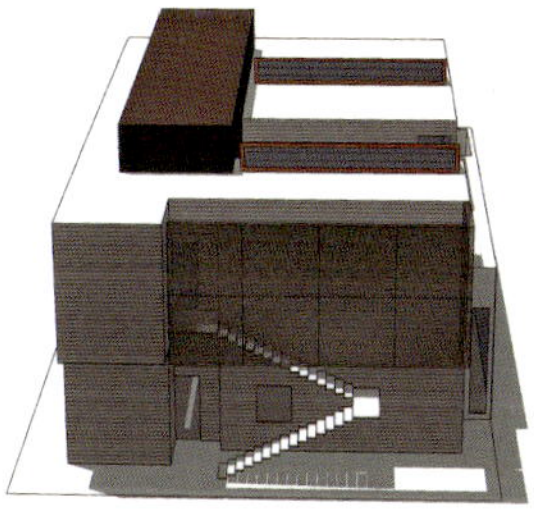

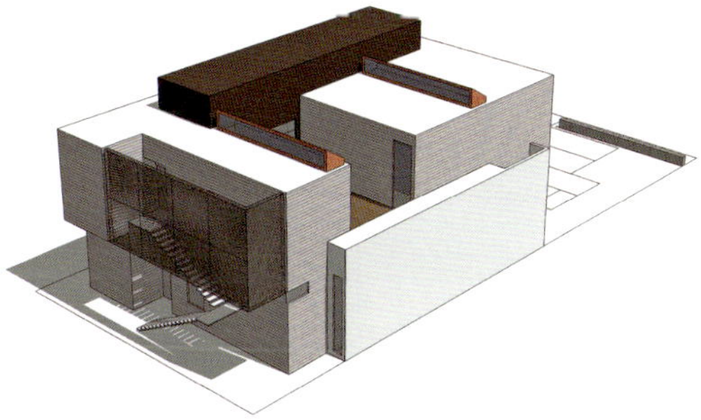

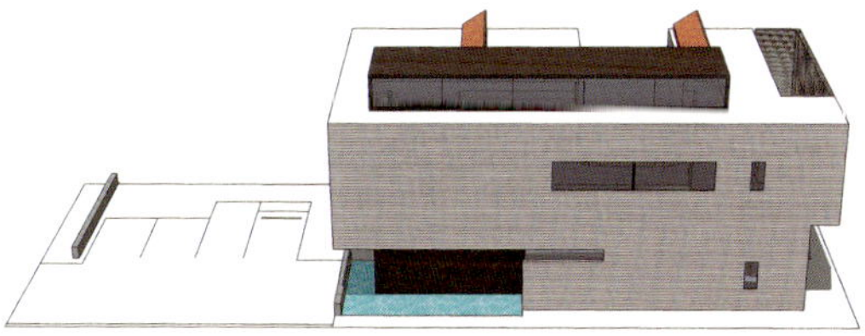

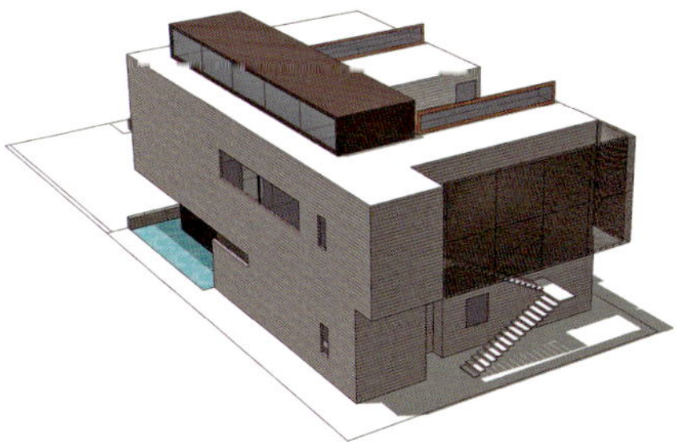

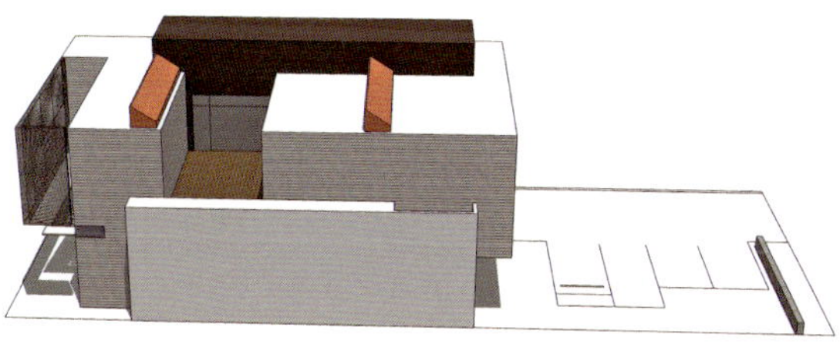

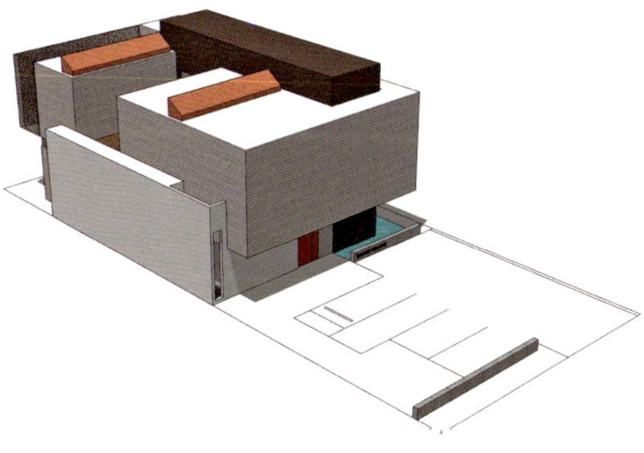

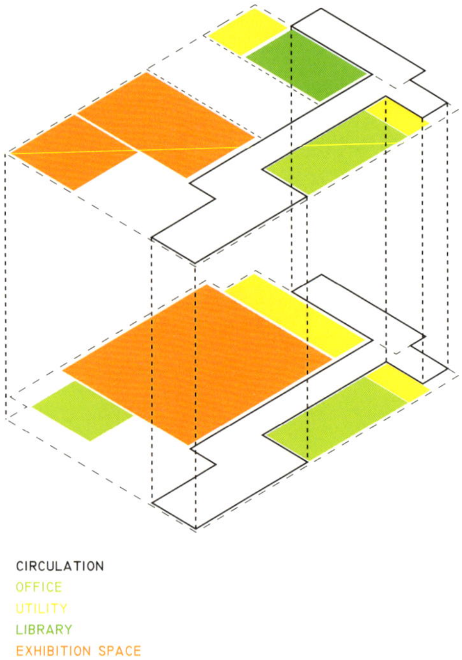
CIRCULATION
OFFICE
UTILITY
LIBRARY
EXHIBITION SPACE

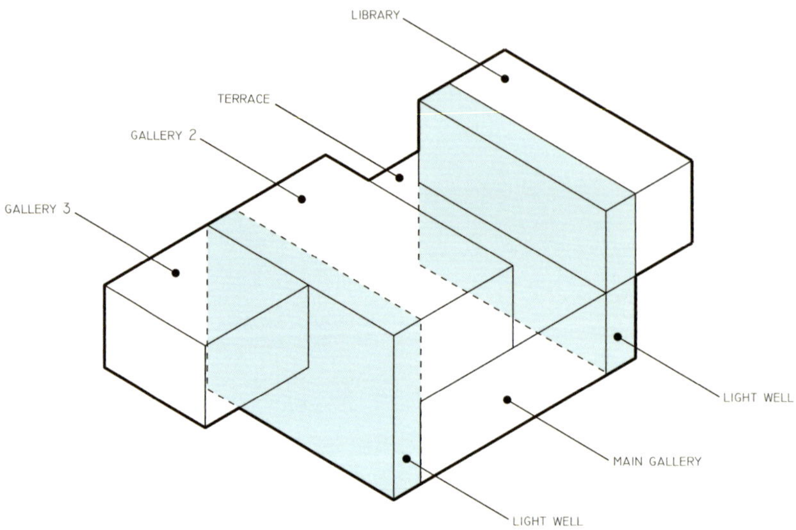
LIBRARY
TERRACE
GALLERY 2
GALLERY 3
LIGHT WELL
MAIN GALLERY
LIGHT WELL

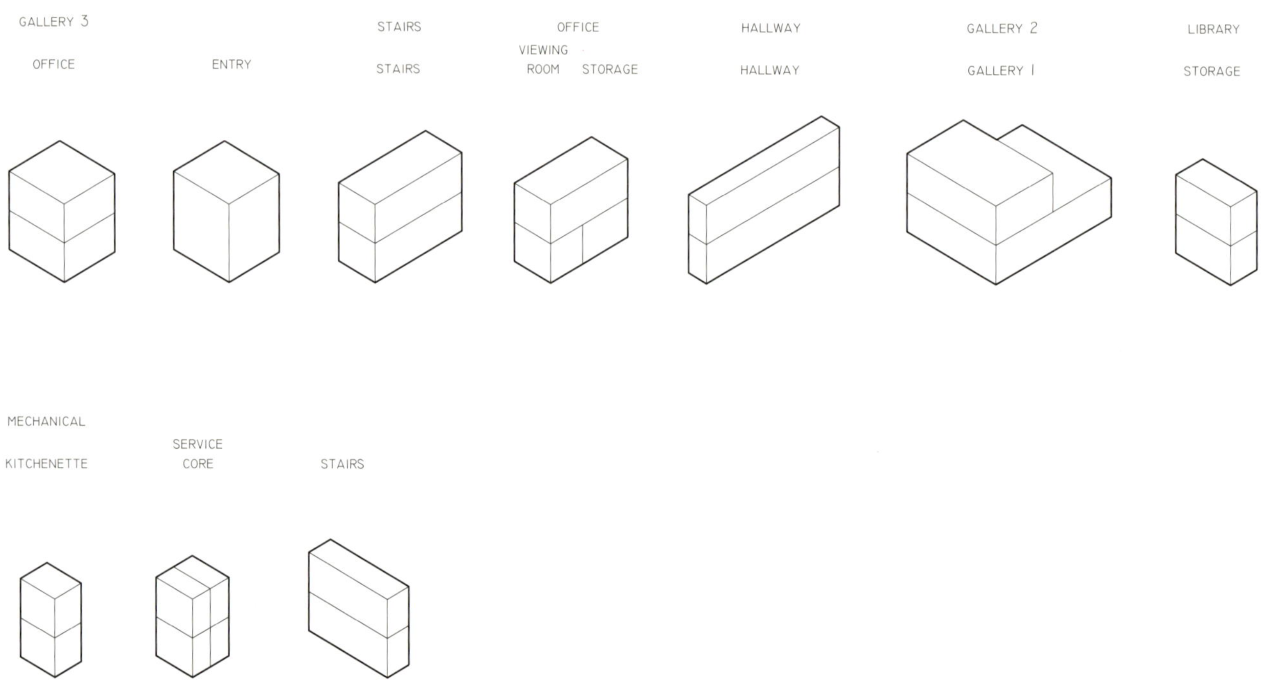
GALLERY 3
OFFICE
ENTRY
STAIRS
STAIRS
OFFICE
VIEWING
ROOM
STORAGE
HALLWAY
HALLWAY
GALLERY 2
GALLERY 1
LIBRARY
STORAGE
MECHANICAL
KITCHENETTE
SERVICE
CORE
STAIRS

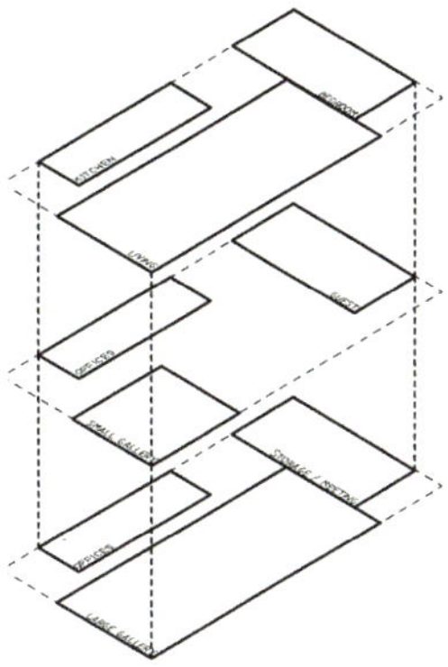

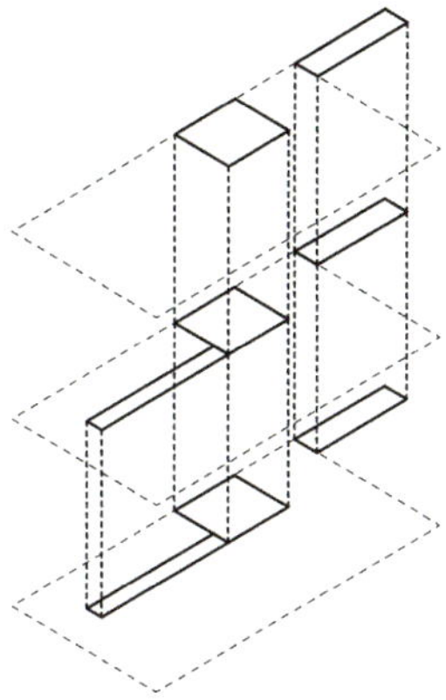

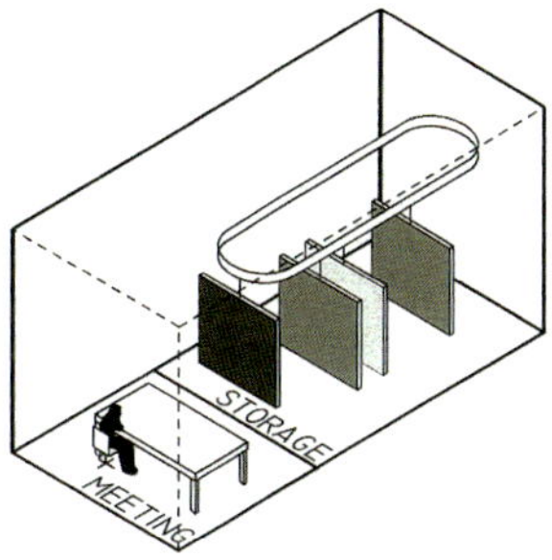
STORAGE
MEETING

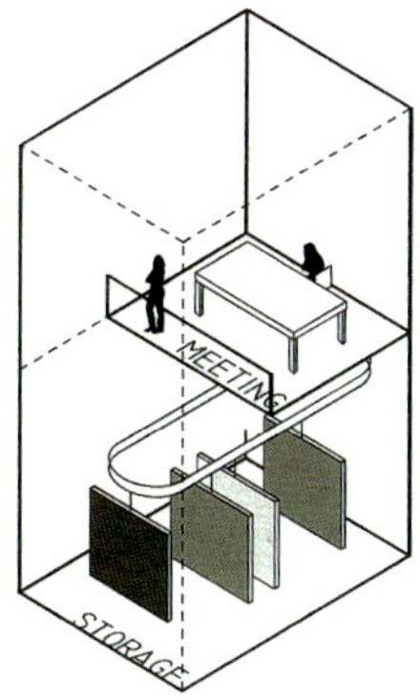
MEETING
STORAGE

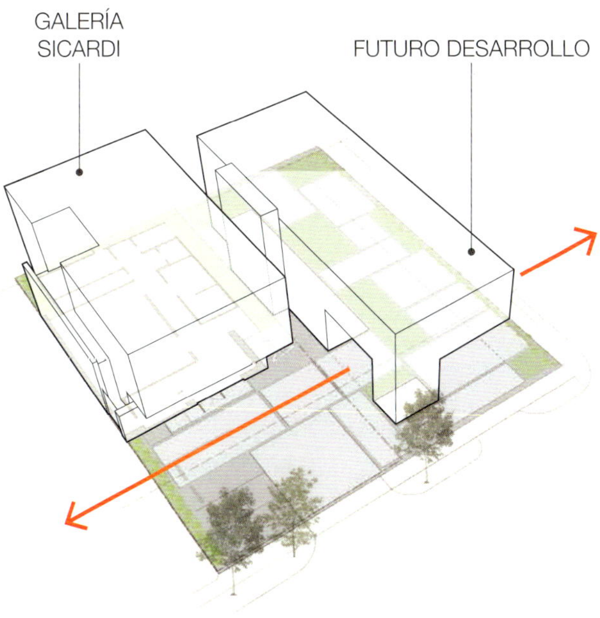
GALERÍA
SICARDI
FUTURO DESARROLLO

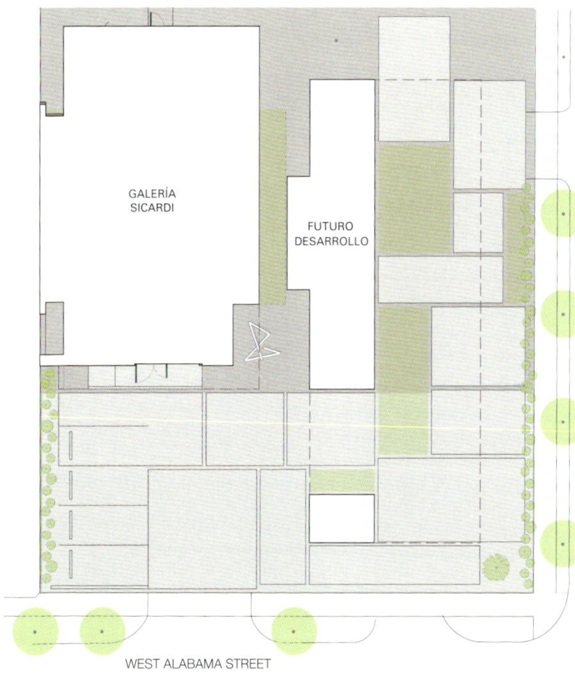
GALERÍA
SICARDI
FUTURO
DESARROLLO
WEST ALABAMA STREET

Models

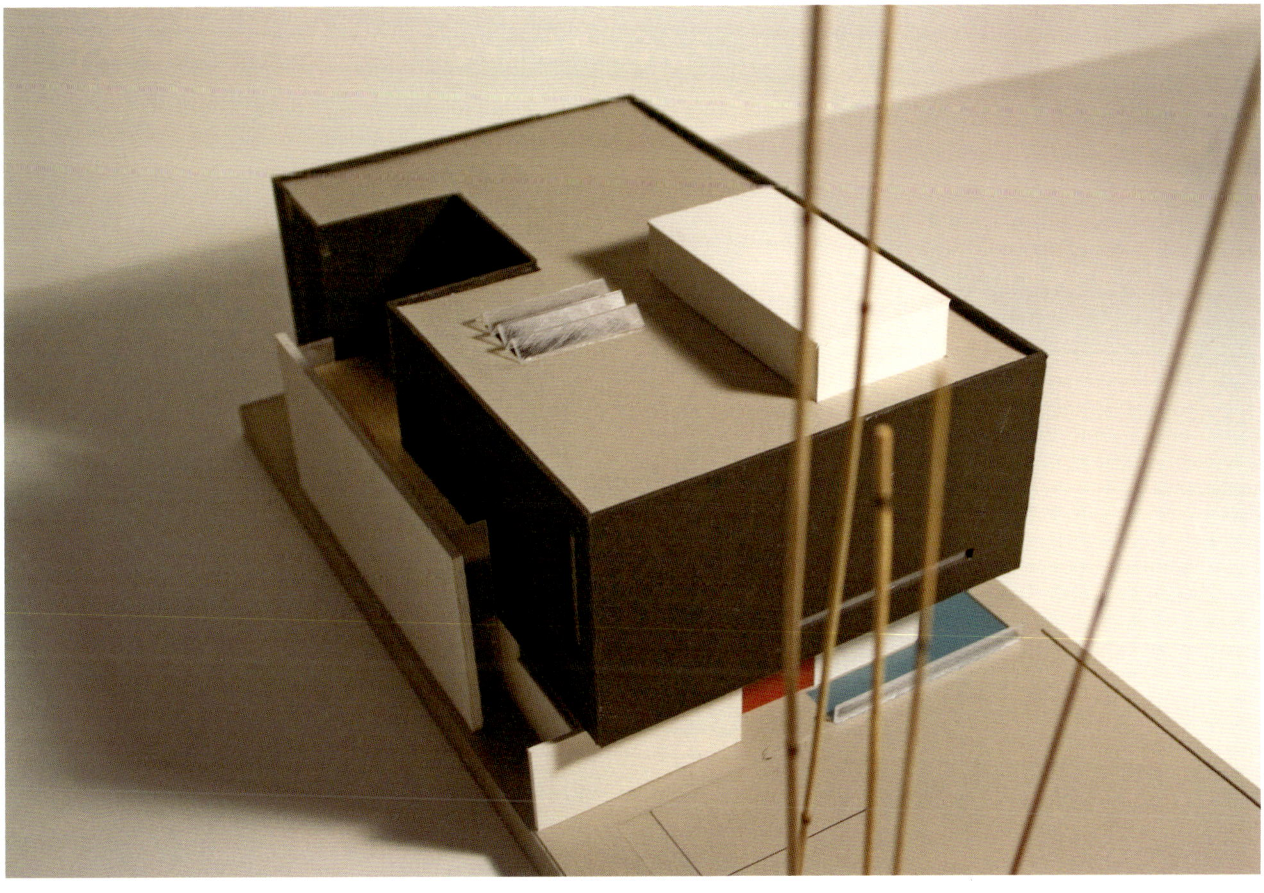

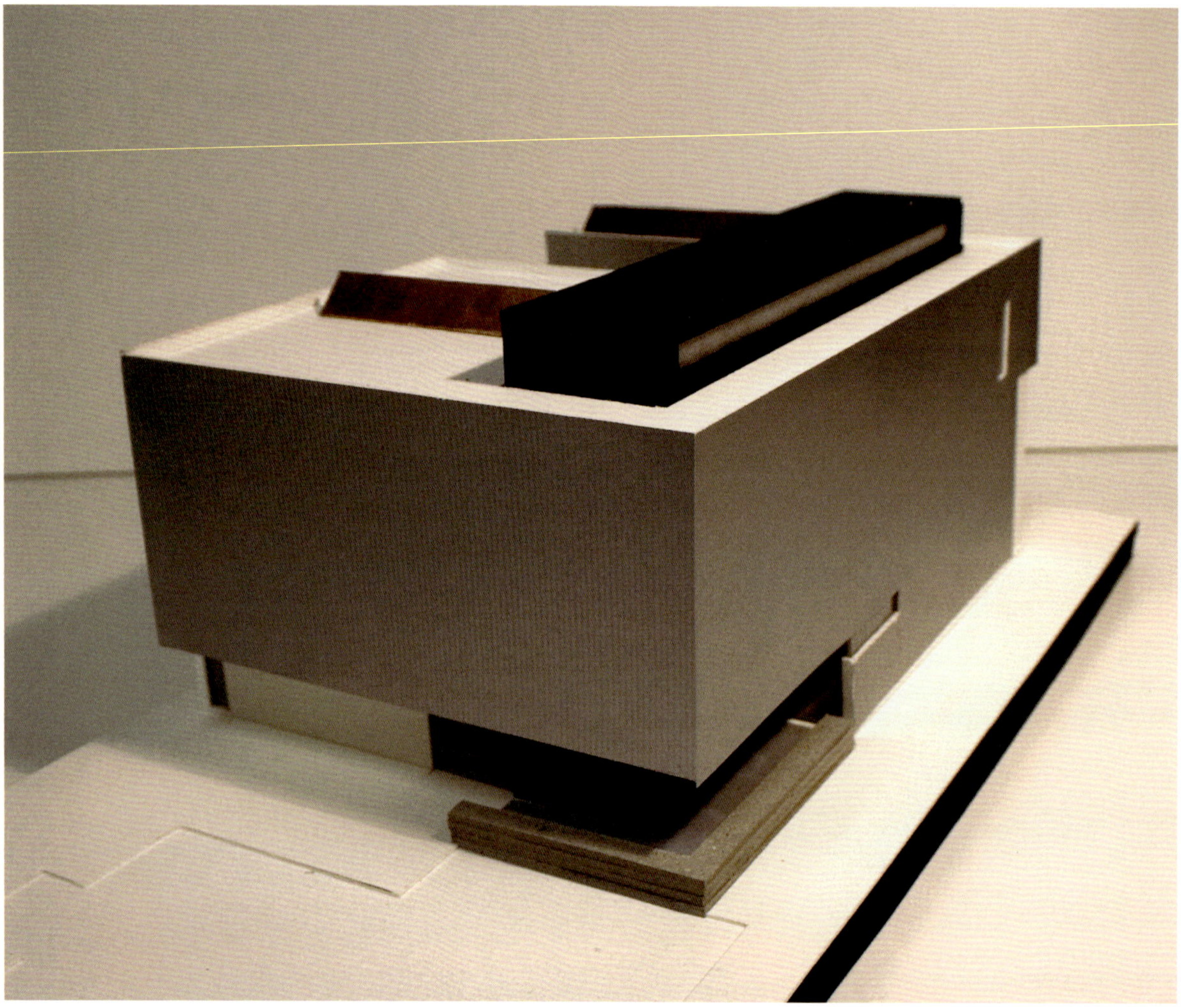

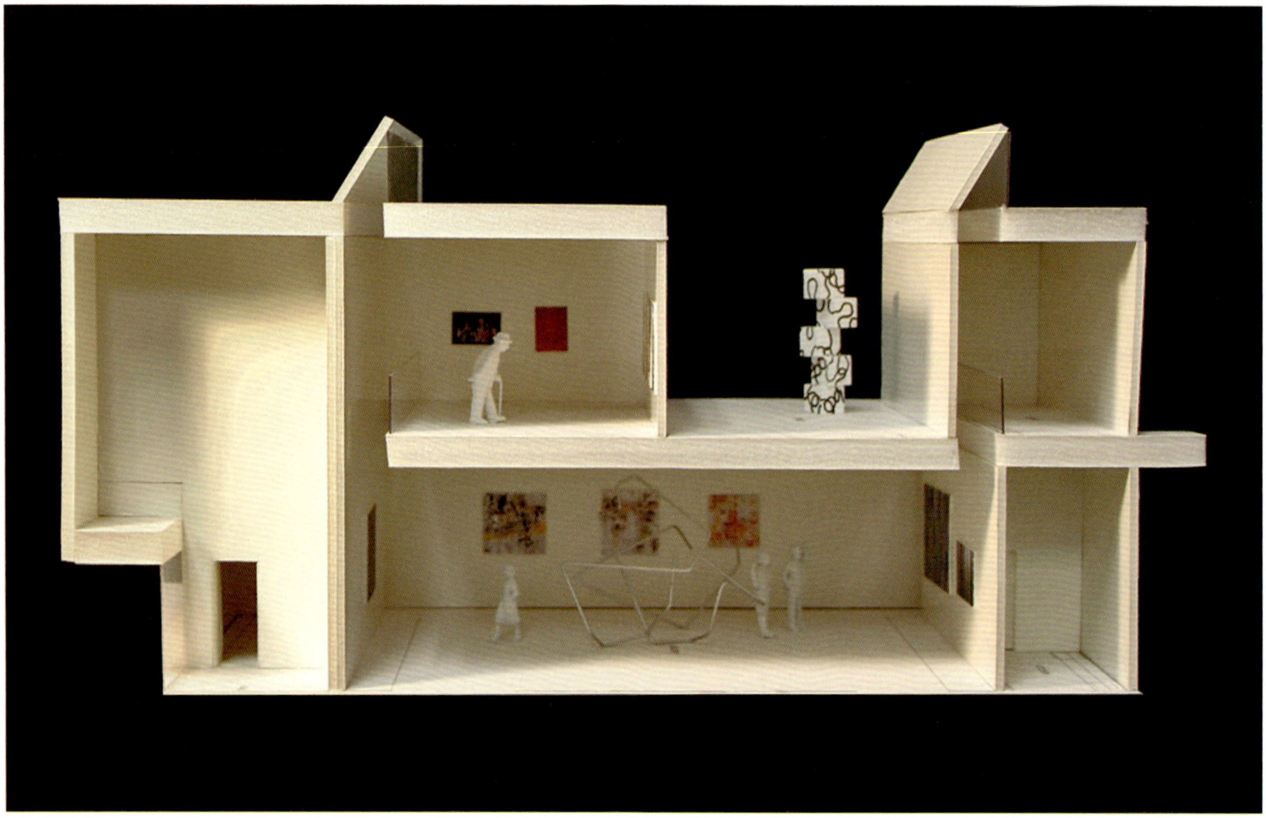

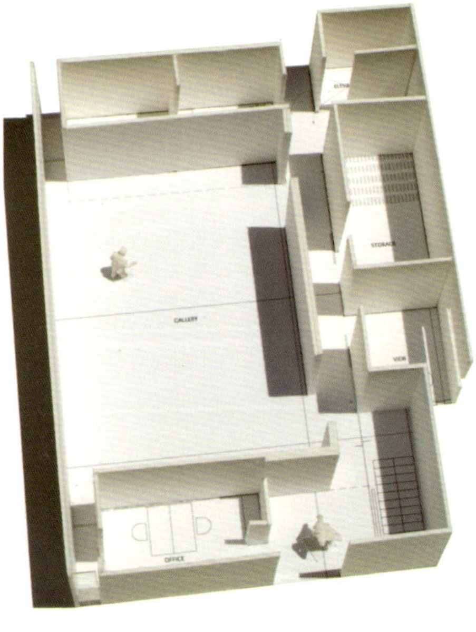
GALLERY
STORAGE
VIEW
OFFICE

LIBRARY
ALLISON
GALLERY 2
HALL
MECHANICAL

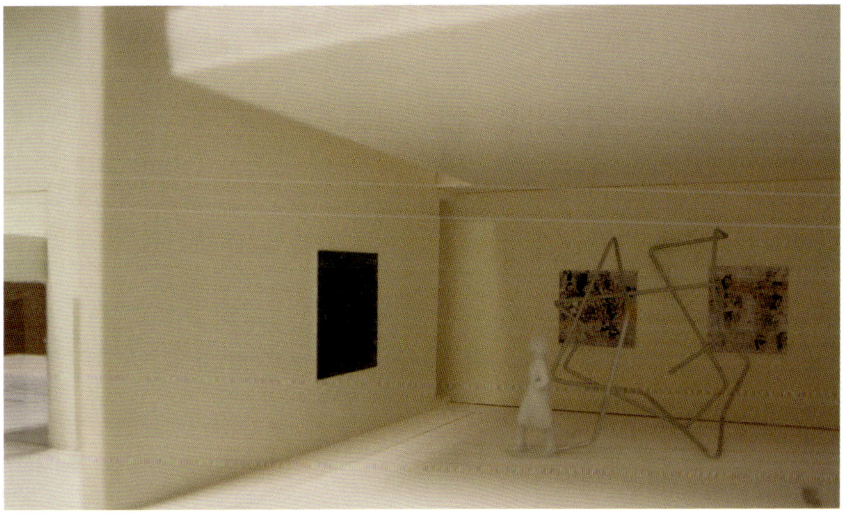

Working Drawings

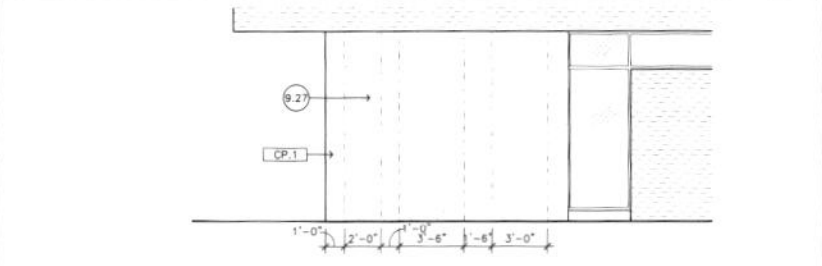

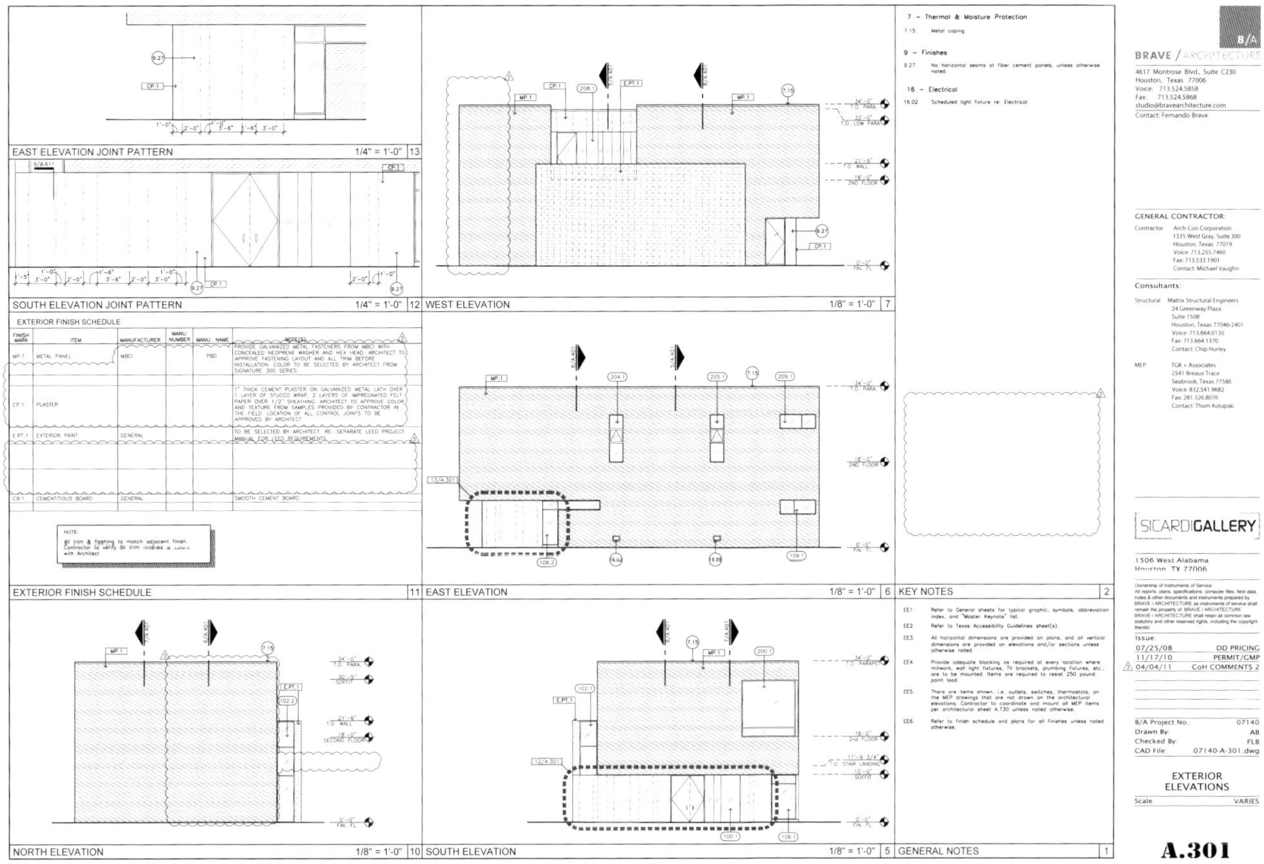

EAST ELEVATION JOINT PATTERN 1/4" = 1'-0" 13

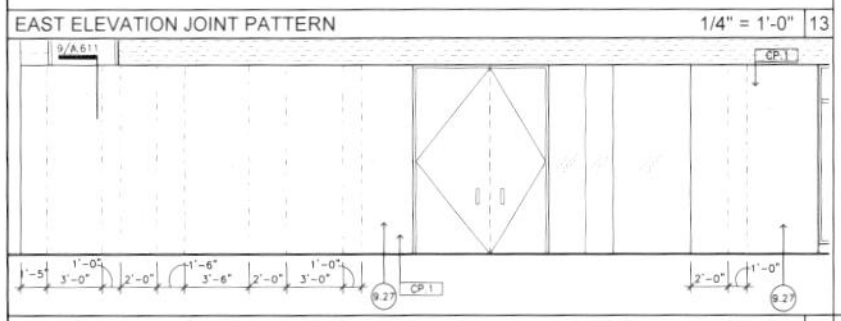

SOUTH ELEVATION JOINT PATTERN 1/4" = 1'-0" 12

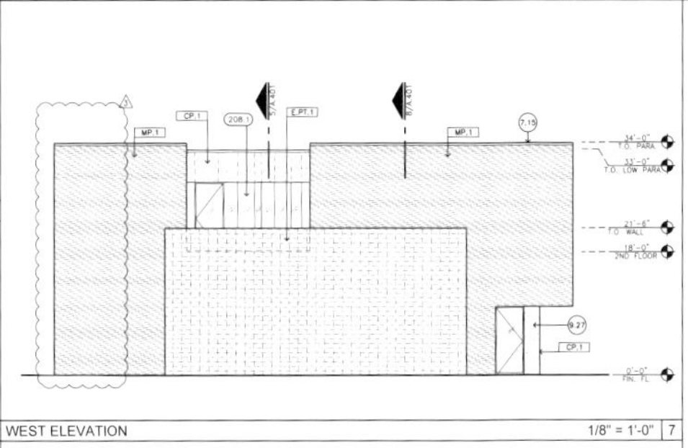

WEST ELEVATION 1/8" = 1'-0" 7

7 – Thermal & Moisture Protection

7.15 Metal coping

9 – Finishes

9.27 No horizontal seams at fiber cement panels, unless otherwise noted.

16 – Electrical

16.02 Scheduled light fixture re: Electrical

EXTERIOR FINISH SCHEDULE

FINISH MARK	ITEM	MANUFACTURER	MANU. NUMBER	MANU. NAME	NOTE(S)
MP.1	METAL PANEL	MBCI		PBD	PROVIDE GALVANIZED METAL FASTENERS FROM MBCI WITH CONCEALED NEOPRENE WASHER AND HEX HEAD. ARCHITECT TO APPROVE FASTENING LAYOUT AND ALL TRIM BEFORE INSTALLATION. COLOR TO BE SELECTED BY ARCHITECT FROM SIGNATURE 300 SERIES.
CP.1	PLASTER				1" THICK CEMENT PLASTER ON GALVANIZED METAL LATH OVER 1 LAYER OF STUCCO WRAP, 2 LAYERS OF IMPREGNATED FELT PAPER OVER 1/2" SHEATHING. ARCHITECT TO APPROVE COLOR AND TEXTURE FROM SAMPLES PROVIDED BY CONTRACTOR IN THE FIELD. LOCATION OF ALL CONTROL JOINTS TO BE APPROVED BY ARCHITECT.
E.PT.1	EXTERIOR PAINT	GENERAL			TO BE SELECTED BY ARCHITECT. RE: SEPARATE LEED PROJECT MANUAL FOR LEED REQUIREMENTS.
CB.1	CEMENTITIOUS BOARD	GENERAL			SMOOTH CEMENT BOARD

NOTE:
All trim & flashing to match adjacent finish. Contractor to verify all trim finishes & colors with Architect

EXTERIOR FINISH SCHEDULE 11

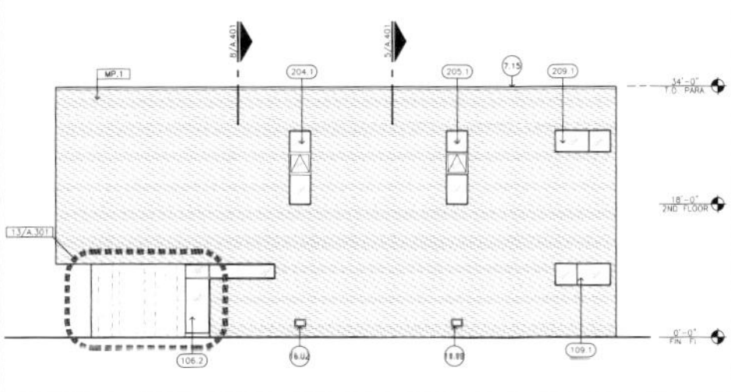

EAST ELEVATION 1/8" = 1'-0" 6

KEY NOTES 2

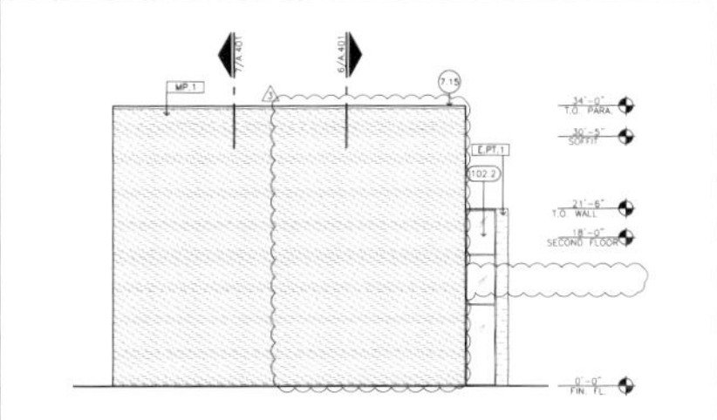

NORTH ELEVATION 1/8" = 1'-0" 10

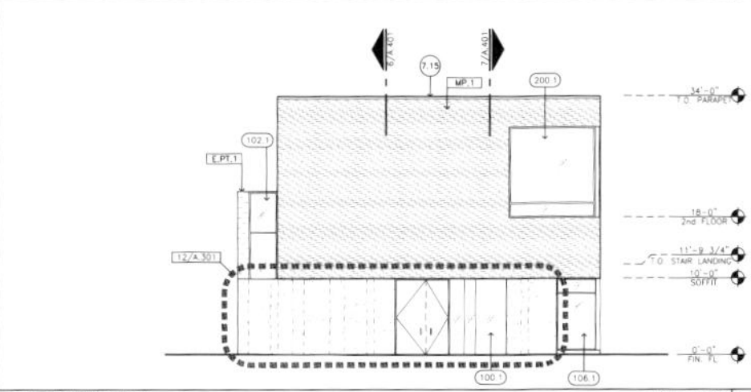

SOUTH ELEVATION 1/8" = 1'-0" 5

EE1. Refer to General sheets for typical graphic, symbols, abbreviation index, and "Master Keynote" list.

EE2. Refer to Texas Accessibility Guidelines sheet(s).

EE3. All horizontal dimensions are provided on plans, and all vertical dimensions are provided on elevations and/or sections unless otherwise noted.

EE4. Provide adequate blocking as required at every location where millwork, wall light fixtures, TV brackets, plumbing fixtures, etc., are to be mounted. Items are required to resist 250 pound point load.

EE5. There are items shown, i.e. outlets, switches, thermostats, on the MEP drawings that are not drawn on the architectural elevations. Contractor to coordinate and mount all MEP items per architectural sheet A.730 unless noted otherwise.

EE6. Refer to finish schedule and plans for all finishes unless noted otherwise.

GENERAL NOTES 1

BRAVE / ARCHITECTURE
4617 Montrose Blvd., Suite C230
Houston, Texas 77006
Voice: 713.524.5858
Fax: 713.524.5868
studio@bravearchitecture.com
Contact: Fernando Brave

GENERAL CONTRACTOR:
Contractor Arch-Con Corporation
1335 West Gray, Suite 300
Houston, Texas 77019
Voice: 713.255.7460
Fax: 713.533.1901
Contact: Michael Vaughn

Consultants:
Structural Matrix Structural Engineers
24 Greenway Plaza
Suite 1508
Houston, Texas 77046-2401
Voice: 713.664.0130
Fax: 713.664.1370
Contact: Chip Hurley

MEP TGK + Associates
2541 Breaux Trace
Seabrook, Texas 77586
Voice: 832.541.9682
Fax: 281.326.8076
Contact: Thom Kolupski

SICARDIGALLERY
1506 West Alabama
Houston, TX 77006

Ownership of Instruments of Service
All reports, plans, specifications, computer files, field data, notes & other documents and instruments prepared by BRAVE / ARCHITECTURE as instruments of service shall remain the property of BRAVE / ARCHITECTURE. BRAVE / ARCHITECTURE shall retain all common law, statutory and other reserved rights, including the copyright thereto.

Issue:
07/25/08 DD PRICING
11/17/10 PERMIT/GMP
3 04/04/11 CoH COMMENTS 2

B/A Project No.: 07140
Drawn By: AB
Checked By: FLB
CAD File: 07140-A-301.dwg

EXTERIOR ELEVATIONS

Scale: VARIES

A.301

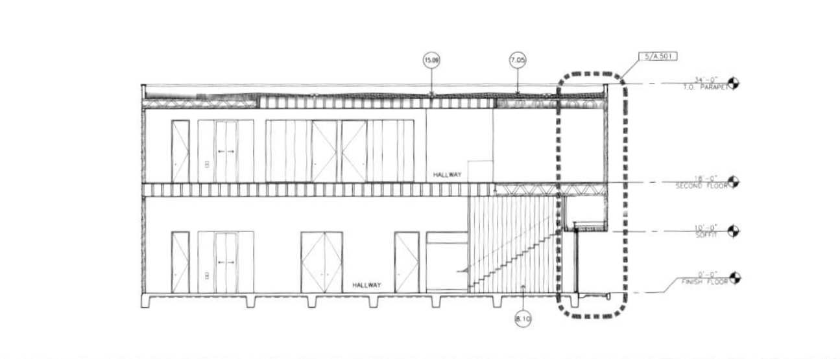

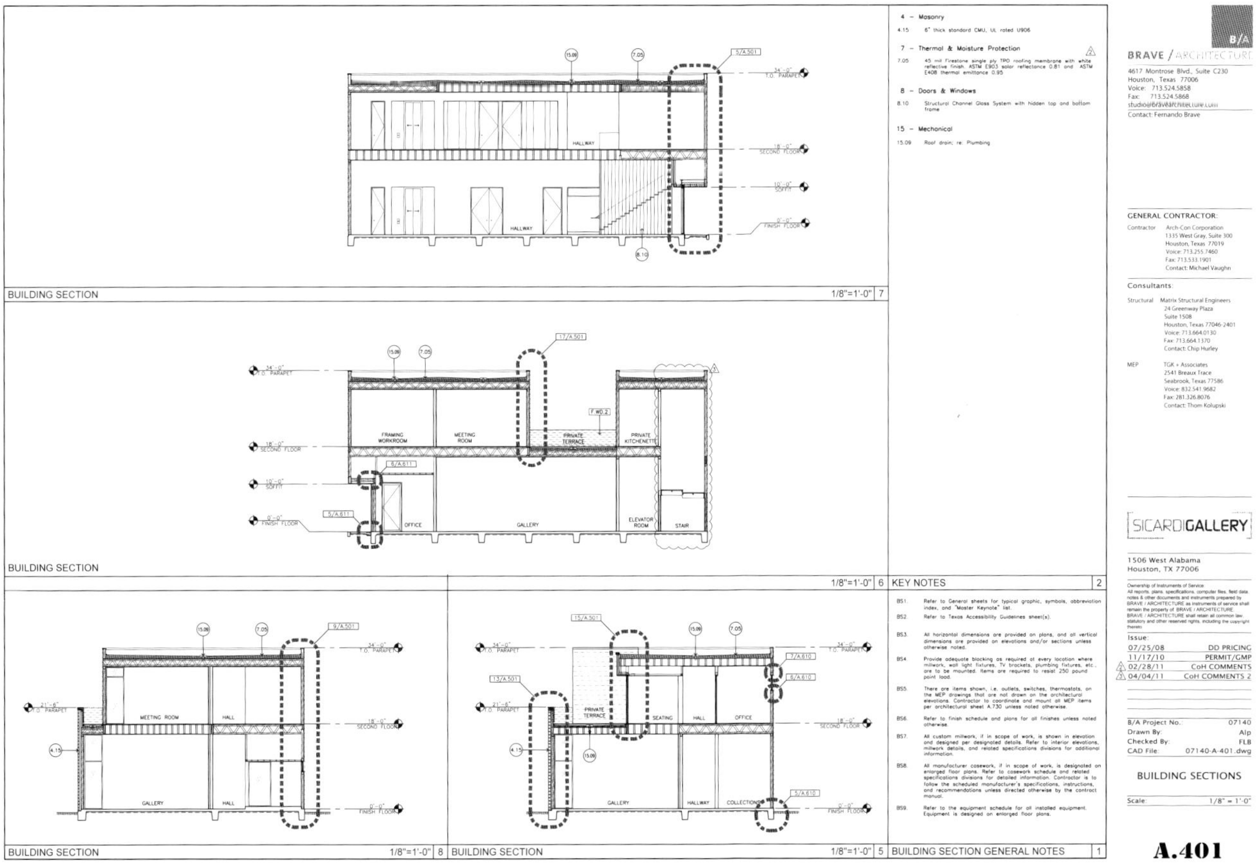

BUILDING SECTION 1/8"=1'-0" 7

4 – Masonry

4.15 6" thick standard CMU, UL rated U906

7 – Thermal & Moisture Protection

7.05 45 mil Firestone single ply TPO roofing membrane with white reflective finish. ASTM E903 solar reflectance 0.81 and ASTM E408 thermal emittance 0.95

8 – Doors & Windows

8.10 Structural Channel Glass System with hidden top and bottom frame

15 – Mechanical

15.09 Roof drain; re: Plumbing

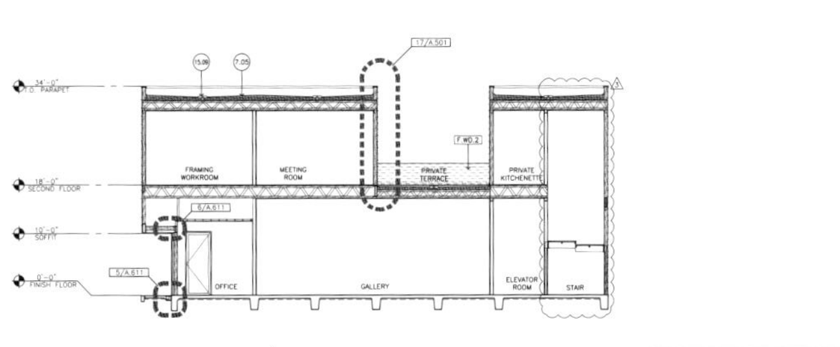

BUILDING SECTION 1/8"=1'-0" 6

KEY NOTES 2

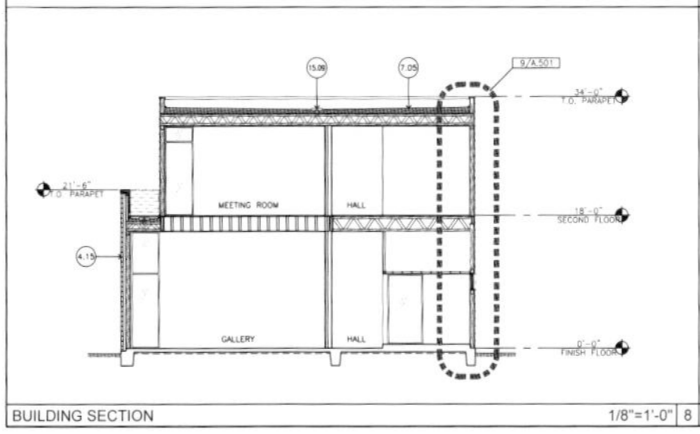

BUILDING SECTION 1/8"=1'-0" 8

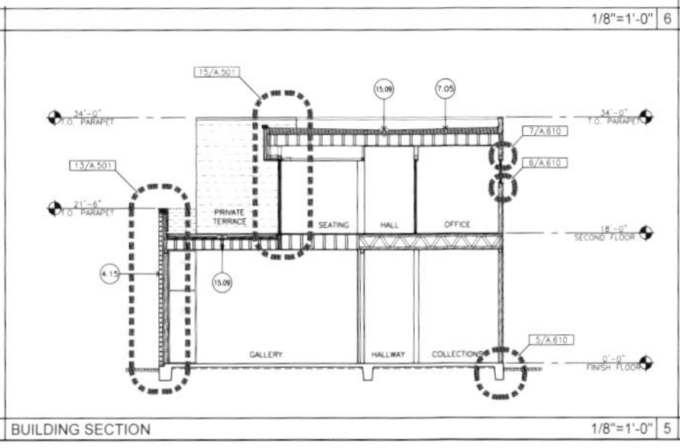

BUILDING SECTION 1/8"=1'-0" 5

BS1. Refer to General sheets for typical graphic, symbols, abbreviation index, and "Master Keynote" list.

BS2. Refer to Texas Accessibility Guidelines sheet(s).

BS3. All horizontal dimensions are provided on plans, and all vertical dimensions are provided on elevations and/or sections unless otherwise noted.

BS4. Provide adequate blocking as required at every location where millwork, wall light fixtures, TV brackets, plumbing fixtures, etc., are to be mounted. Items are required to resist 250 pound point load.

BS5. There are items shown, i.e. outlets, switches, thermostats, on the MEP drawings that are not drawn on the architectural elevations. Contractor to coordinate and mount all MEP items per architectural sheet A.730 unless noted otherwise.

BS6. Refer to finish schedule and plans for all finishes unless noted otherwise.

BS7. All custom millwork, if in scope of work, is shown in elevation and designed per designated details. Refer to interior elevations, millwork details, and related specifications divisions for additional information.

BS8. All manufacturer casework, if in scope of work, is designated on enlarged floor plans. Refer to casework schedule and related specifications divisions for detailed information. Contractor is to follow the scheduled manufacturer's specifications, instructions, and recommendations unless directed otherwise by the contract manual.

BS9. Refer to the equipment schedule for all installed equipment. Equipment is designed on enlarged floor plans.

BUILDING SECTION GENERAL NOTES 1

BRAVE / ARCHITECTURE
4617 Montrose Blvd., Suite C230
Houston, Texas 77006
Voice: 713.524.5858
Fax: 713.524.5868
studio@bravearchitecture.com
Contact: Fernando Brave

GENERAL CONTRACTOR:
Contractor Arch-Con Corporation
1335 West Gray, Suite 300
Houston, Texas 77019
Voice: 713.255.7460
Fax: 713.533.1901
Contact: Michael Vaughn

Consultants:
Structural Matrix Structural Engineers
24 Greenway Plaza
Suite 1508
Houston, Texas 77046-2401
Voice: 713.664.0130
Fax: 713.664.1370
Contact: Chip Hurley

MEP TGK + Associates
2541 Breaux Trace
Seabrook, Texas 77586
Voice: 832.541.9682
Fax: 281.326.8076
Contact: Thom Kolupski

SICARDIGALLERY
1506 West Alabama
Houston, TX 77006

Ownership of Instruments of Service
All reports, plans, specifications, computer files, field data, notes & other documents and instruments prepared by BRAVE / ARCHITECTURE as instruments of service shall remain the property of BRAVE / ARCHITECTURE. BRAVE / ARCHITECTURE shall retain all common law, statutory and other reserved rights, including the copyright thereto.

Issue:
07/25/08 DD PRICING
11/17/10 PERMIT/GMP
2 02/28/11 CoH COMMENTS
3 04/04/11 CoH COMMENTS 2

B/A Project No.: 07140
Drawn By: Alp
Checked By: FLB
CAD File: 07140-A-401.dwg

BUILDING SECTIONS

Scale: 1/8" = 1'-0"

A.401

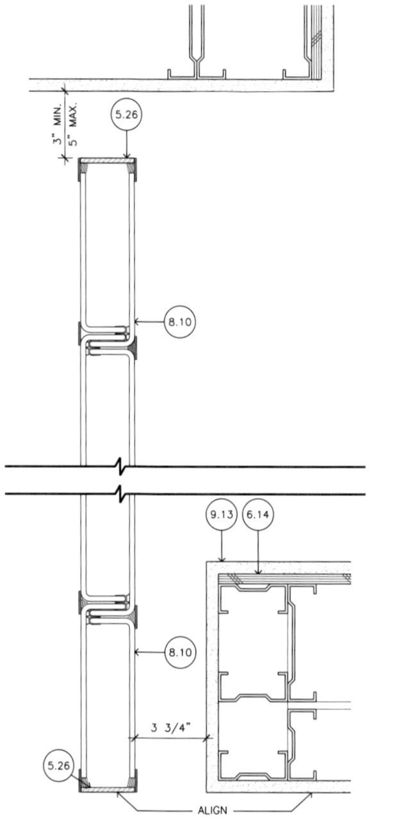

PLAN DETAIL 3" = 1'-0" 15

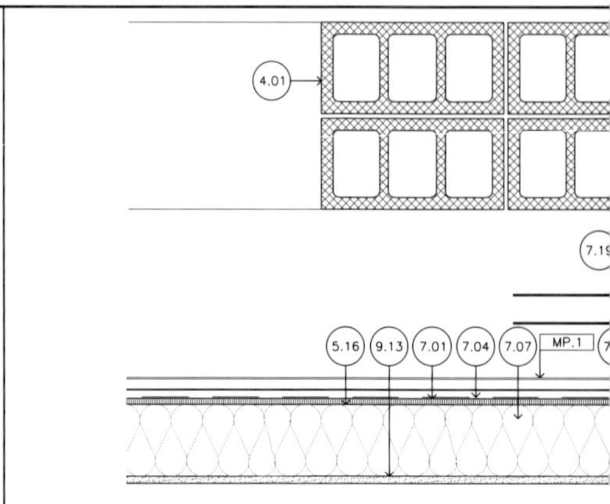

PLAN DETAIL

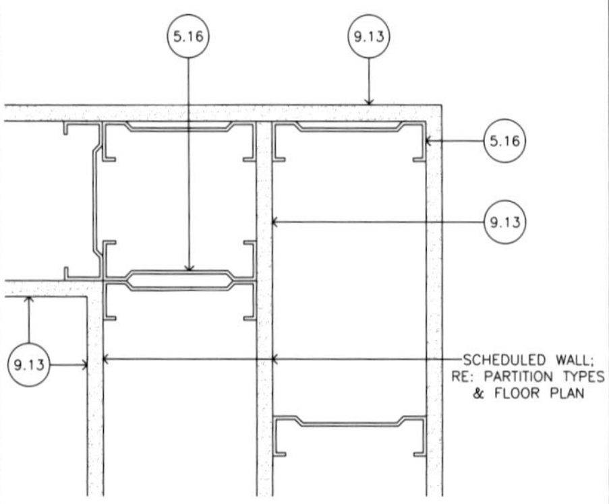

PLAN DETAIL 3" = 1'-0" 19

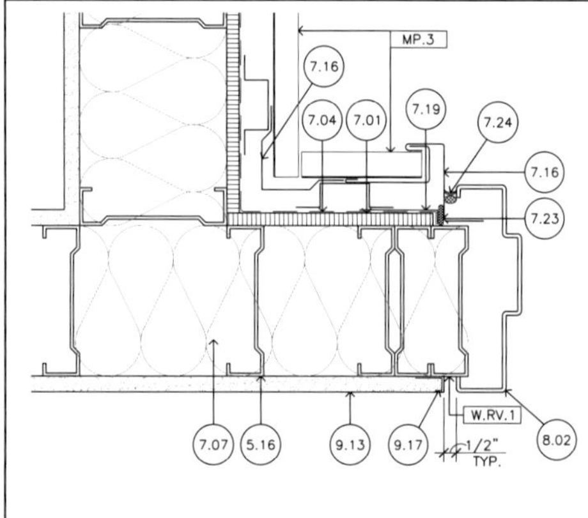

PLAN DETAIL 3" = 1'-0" 11

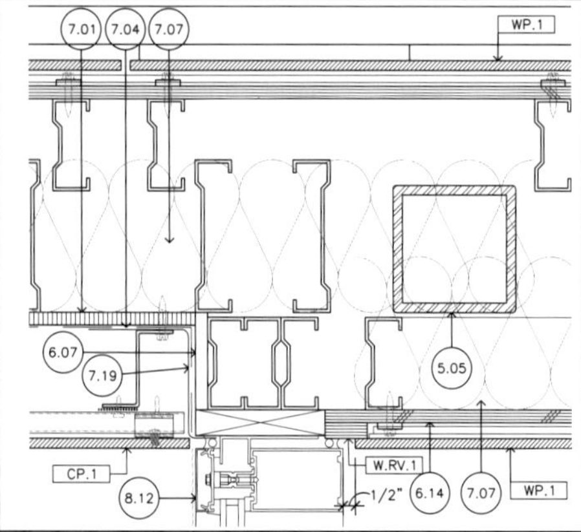

PLAN DETAIL 3" = 1'-0" 18

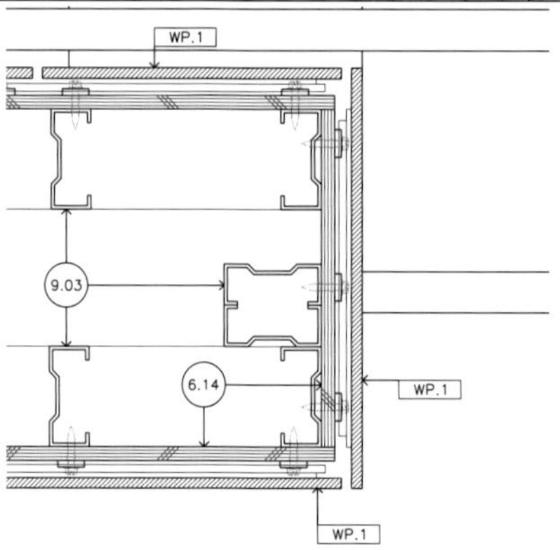

PLAN DETAIL 3" = 1'-0" 14

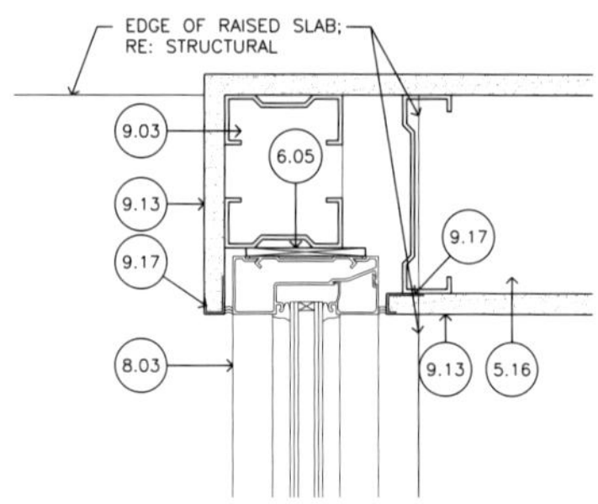

PLAN DETAIL 3" = 1'-0" 10

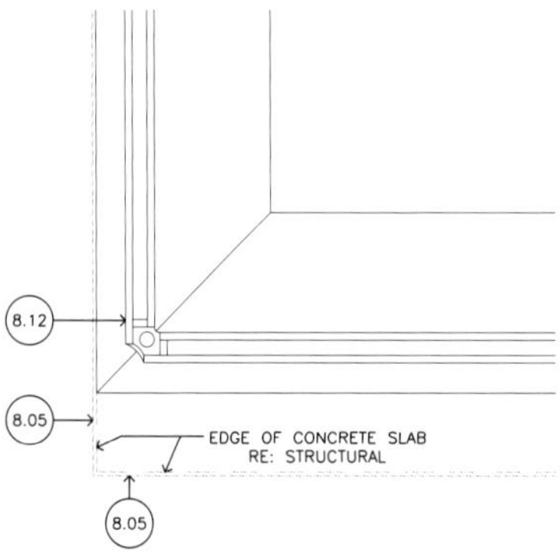

PLAN DETAIL 3" = 1'-0" 17

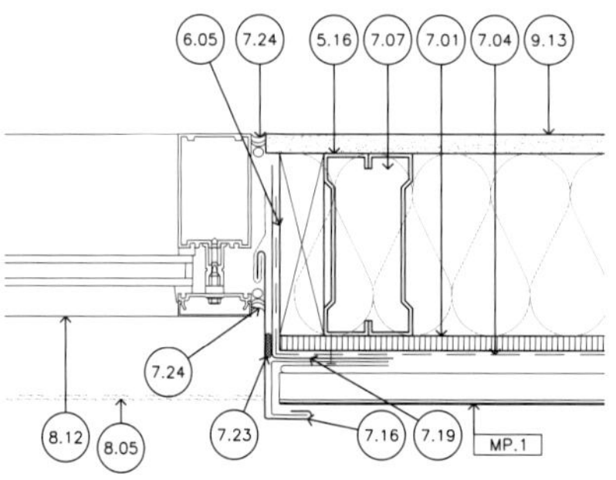

PLAN DETAIL 3" = 1'-0" 13

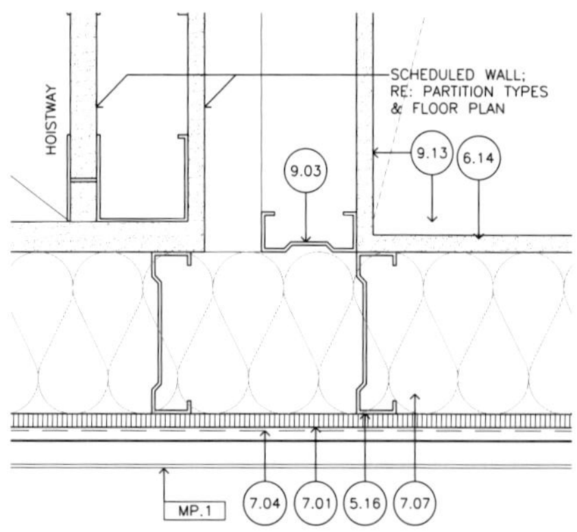

PLAN DETAIL 3" = 1'-0" 9

PL
TY
PL

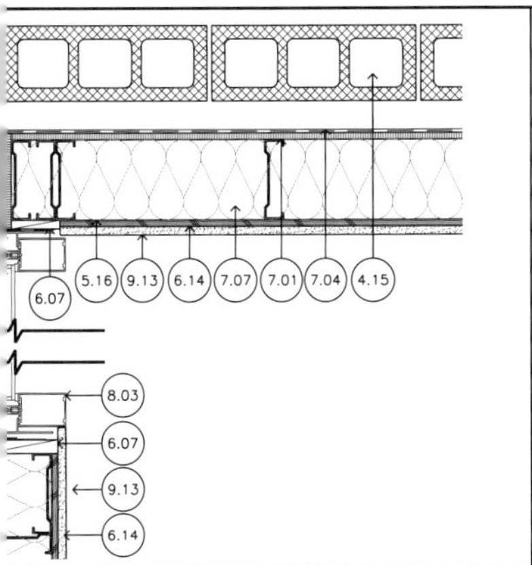

1-1/2"=1'-0" | 11

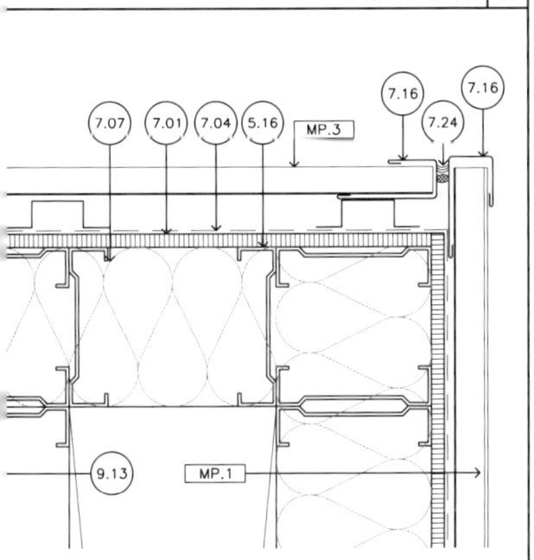

'AIL | 3" = 1'-0" | 7

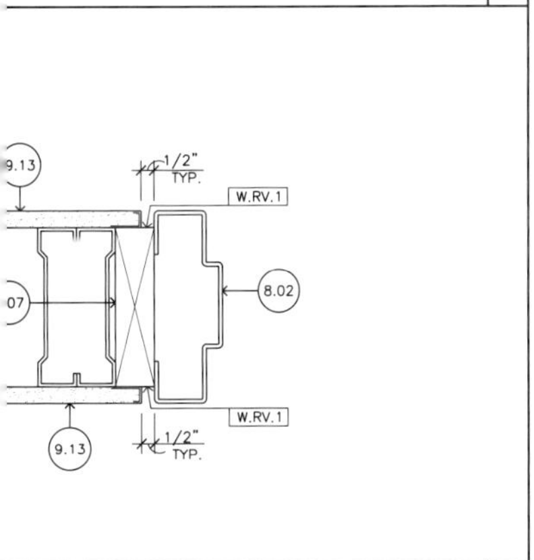

REVEAL @ DOOR | 3" = 1'-0" | 6

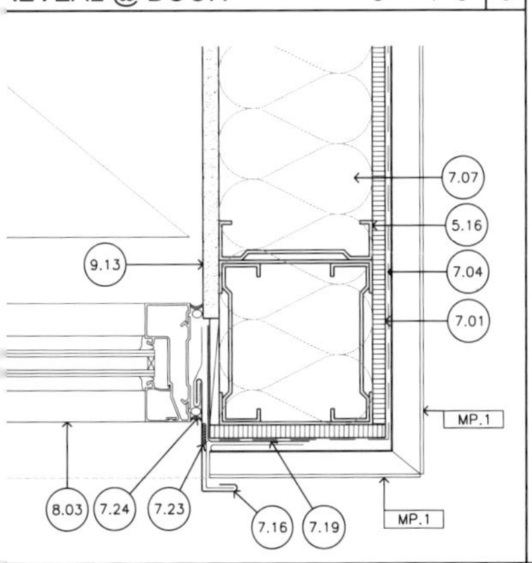

'AIL | 3" = 1'-0" | 5

KEY NOTES | 1

3 – Concrete

3.01 Concrete slab; re: Structural

4 – Masonry

4.01 8" thick standard CMU, UL Rated
4.08 Weep holes @ 24" O.C. Max
4.14 Cast Stone
4.15 6" thick standard CMU, UL rated U906

5 – Metals

5.02 Steel beam; re: Structural
5.04 Steel deck; re: Structural
5.05 Steel tube; re: Structural
5.06 Steel angle; re: Structural
5.16 6" galvanized CFMF; re: Structural
5.23 4" Galv. CFMF
5.24 Zinc Coping to match exterior metal finish
5.25 Metal Coping
5.26 1/4" steel plate jamb. Install per structural glass manufacturer's recommendations
5.27 Metal Panel. Painted, color to be selected by Architect

6 – Wood & Plastics

6.02 2" x treated continuous blocking
6.05 Shim as required
6.07 Treated wood blocking as required
6.09 Continuous fiber cant strip
6.14 1/2" Plywood

7 – Thermal & Moisture Protection

7.01 1/2" Densglass sheathing
7.04 Dampproofing
7.05 Heat adhered modified bitumen roof. Solar reflectance index to be .78 minimum.
7.07 6" batt insulation
7.10 4" base rigid board Insulation
7.16 Metal trim flashing
7.19 Window tape flashing
7.20 Tapered insulation
7.23 Sealant
7.24 Sealant and backer rod
7.26 Standing seam metal roof
7.29 Continuous cleat
7.35 Flashing
7.36 Continuous ice & water shield
7.37 Base flashing

8 – Doors & Windows

8.02 Scheduled door frame
8.03 Scheduled window
8.05 Continuous soldered sill pan with end dams on a bed of mastic. finish to match window frame.
8.10 Structural Channel Glass System with hidden top and bottom frame
8.12 Double insulated glass with mitered frame and structural silicone butt joint; Re: Window Schedule

9 – Finishes

9.03 3-5/8" metal studs at 16" O.C. Maximum
9.13 5/8" Type X gypsum board
9.17 Paper faced metal "J" Corner bead
9.19 Ceiling drop panel projector mount. Location to be coordinated with Architect
9.20 Wood flooring system
9.20 Metal stud bracing as required

10 – Specialties

10.09 Ipe wood roof decking system mounted on sleepers over built-up roof system. All wood to be treated. Architect to approve all decking and fastening layouts.Provide equipment pads under all wood deck runners to be supported on roofing
10.14 Sail cloth fabric system attached to wall at clerestory

11 – Equipment

11.02 Ceiling-mounted electrical drop down rear-projection screen
11.03 Ceiling-mounted electrical drop down front-projection screen

15 – Mechanical

15.09 Roof drain; re: Plumbing

16 – Electrical

16.02 Scheduled light fixture re: Electrical

RE: 11/A.301 FOR EXTERIOR FINISH SCHEDULE
RE: 3/A.151 FOR INTERIOR FINISH SCHEDULE

NOTE: G.C. TO COORDINATE FINISH MATERIAL & TRIM/FLASHING FINISHES & VERIFY WITH ARCHITECT

B/A
BRAVE / ARCHITECTURE
4617 Montrose Blvd., Suite C230
Houston, Texas 77006
Voice: 713.524.5858
Fax: 713.524.5868
studio@bravearchitecture.com
Contact: Fernando Brave

Consultants:

Structural: Matrix Structural Engineers
24 Greenway Plaza
Suite 1508
Houston, Texas 77046-2401
Voice: 713.664.0130
Fax: 713.664.1370
Contact: Chip Hurley

MEP: TGK + Associates
2541 Breaux Trace
Seabrook, Texas 77586
Voice: 832.541.9682
Fax: 281.326.8076
Contact: Thom Kolupski

LEED: Rice & Gardner Consultants, Inc.
6161 Savoy Drive, Suite 1212
Houston, Texas 77036
Voice: 713.482.2300
Fax: 713.482.2314
Contact: James Thornton

SICARDIGALLERY

1506 West Alabama
Houston, TX 77006

Issue:
11/17/10 PERMIT / GMP

B/A Project No.: 07140
Drawn By: Alp
Checked By: FLB
CAD File: 07140-A-101.dwg

PLAN DETAILS

Scale: VARIES

A.601

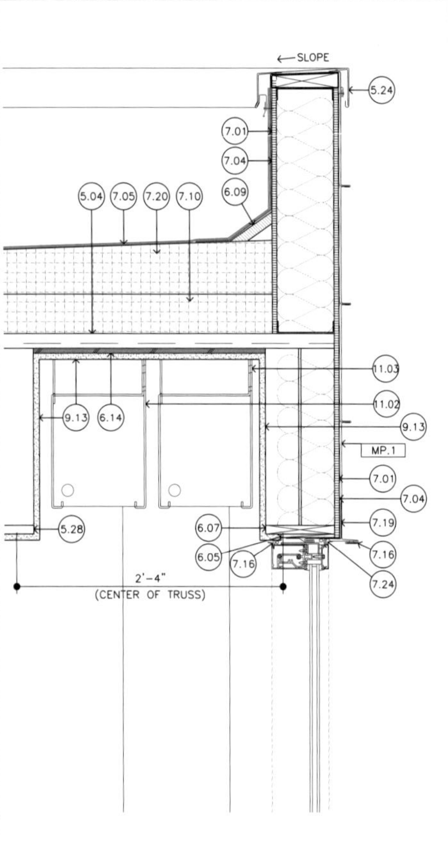

DETAIL 1-1/2"=1'-0" 19

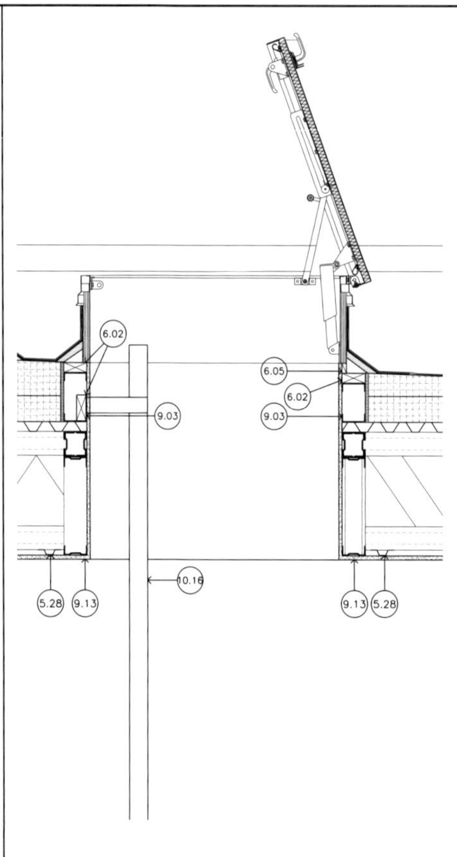

DETAIL 1"=1'-0" 15

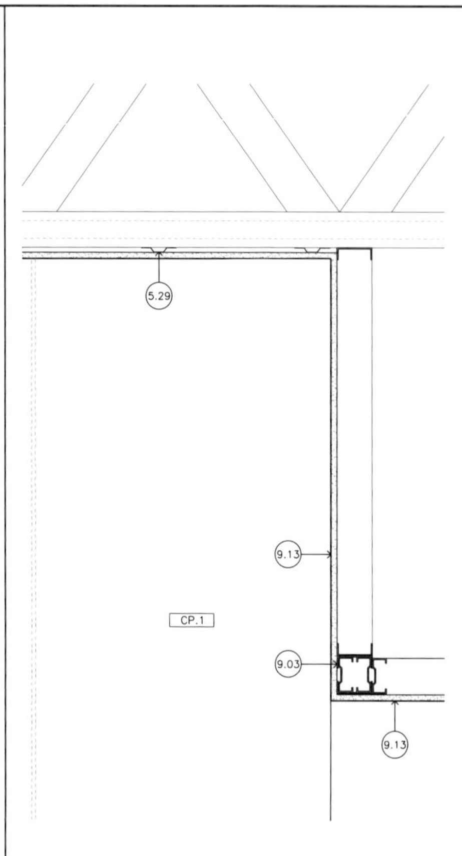

DETAIL 1-1/2"=1'-0" 11

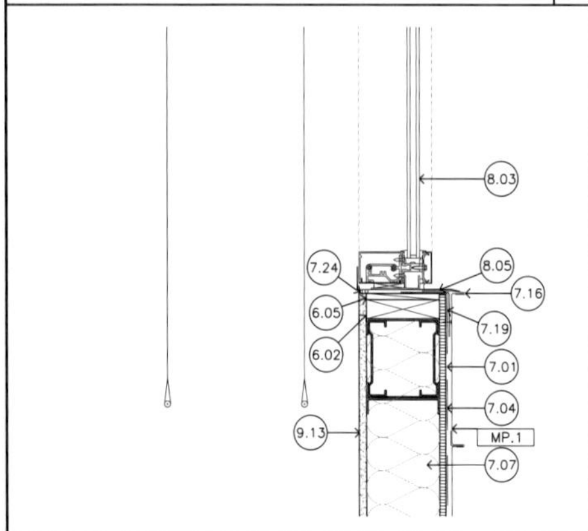

DETAIL 1-1/2"=1'-0" 18

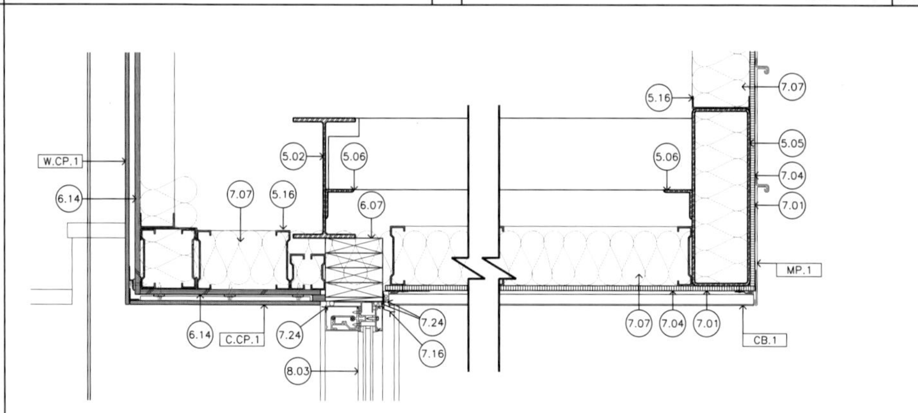

DETAIL 1-1/2"=1'-0" 10

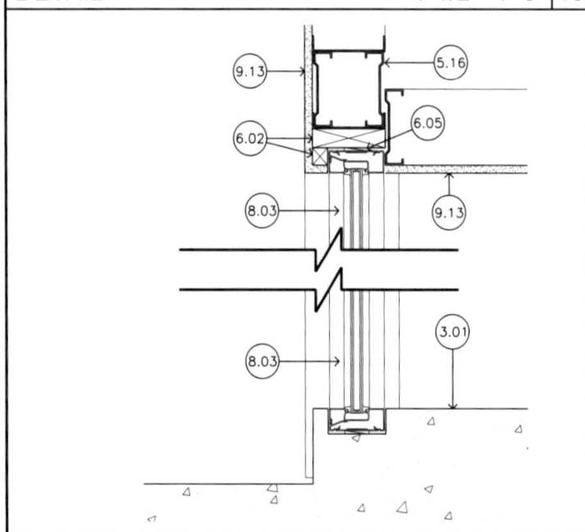

DETAIL 1-1/2"=1'-0" 17

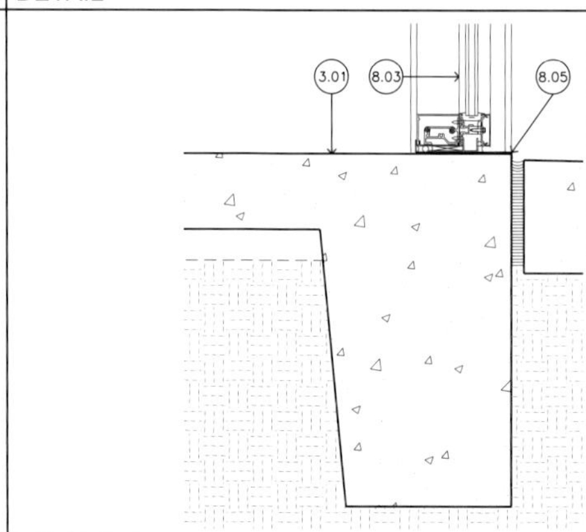

DETAIL 1-1/2"=1'-0" 13

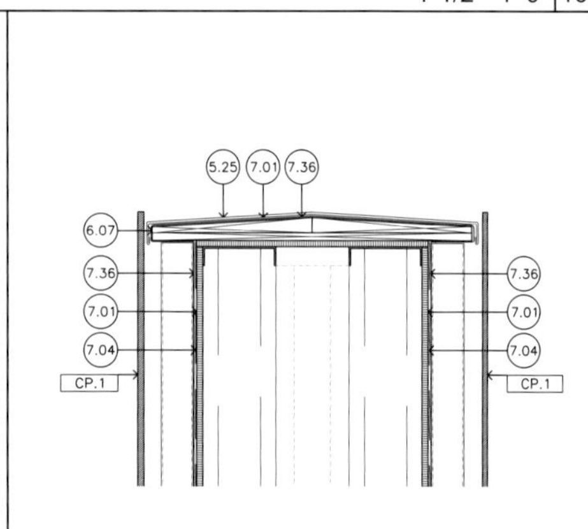

DETAIL 1-1/2"=1'-0" 9

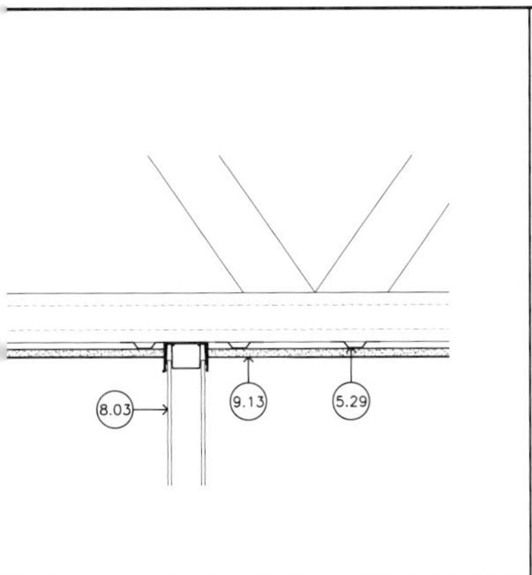

1-1/2"=1'-0" | 8

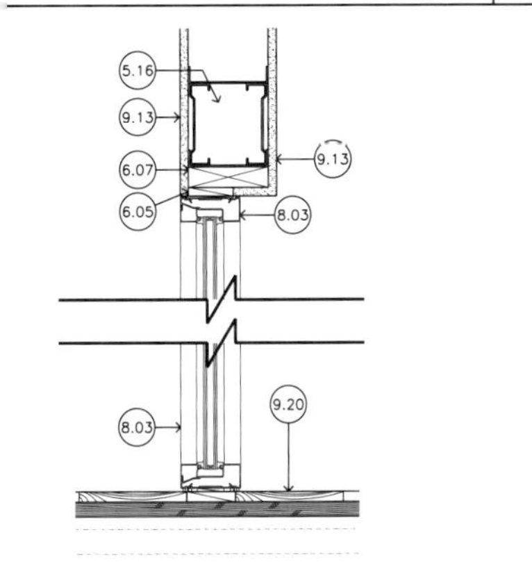

1-1/2"=1'-0" | 7

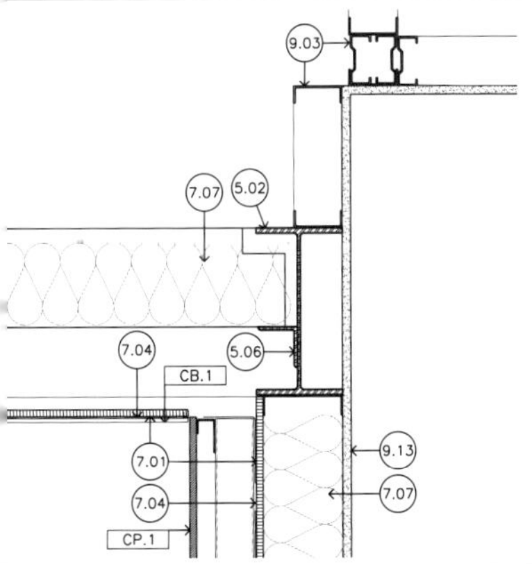

1-1/2"=1'-0" | 6

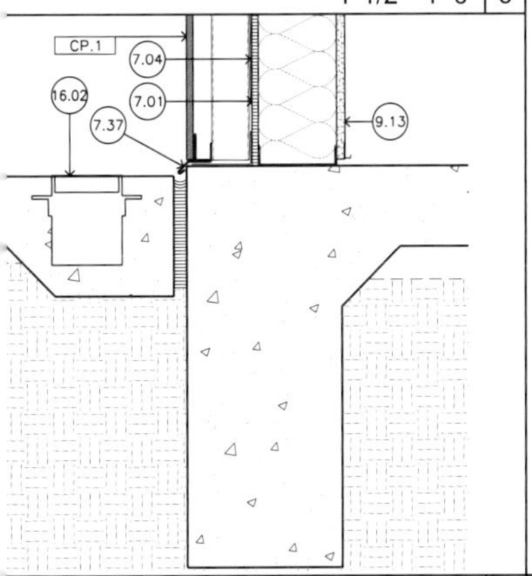

1-1/2"=1'-0" | 5

3 – Concrete

3.01 Concrete slab; re: Structural

4 – Masonry

4.08 Weep holes @ 24" O.C. Max
4.14 Cast Stone
4.15 6" thick standard CMU, UL rated U906

5 – Metals

5.02 Steel beam; re: Structural
5.04 Steel deck; re: Structural
5.05 Steel tube; re: Structural
5.06 Steel angle; re: Structural
5.16 6" galvanized CFMF; re: Structural
5.23 4" Galv. CFMF
5.24 Zinc Coping to match exterior metal finish
5.25 Metal Coping
5.28 7/8" steel furring channels; re: Structural
5.29 1/2" steel furring channels; re: Structural

6 – Wood & Plastics

6.02 2" x treated continuous blocking
6.05 Shim as required
6.07 Treated wood blocking as required
6.09 Continuous fiber cant strip
6.14 1/2" Plywood

7 – Thermal & Moisture Protection

7.01 1/2" Densglass sheathing
7.04 Dampproofing
7.05 Heat adhered modified bitumen roof. Solar reflectance index to be .78 minimum.
7.07 6" batt insulation
7.10 4" base rigid board Insulation
7.16 Metal trim flashing
7.19 Window tape flashing
7.20 Tapered insulation
7.23 Sealant
7.24 Sealant and backer rod
7.26 Standing seam metal roof
7.29 Continuous cleat
7.35 Flashing
7.36 Continuous ice & water shield
7.37 Base flashing

8 – Doors & Windows

8.03 Scheduled window
8.05 Continuous soldered sill pan with end dams on a bed of mastic. finish to match window frame.

9 – Finishes

9.03 3-5/8" metal studs at 16" O.C. Maximum
9.13 5/8" Type X gypsum board
9.17 Paper faced metal "J" Corner bead
9.19 Ceiling drop panel projector mount. Location to be coordinated with Architect
9.20 Wood flooring system
9.26 Metal stud bracing as required

10 – Specialties

10.09 Ipe wood roof decking system mounted on sleepers over built-up roof system. All wood to be treated. Architect to approve all decking and fastening layouts.Provide equipment pads under all wood deck runners to be supported on roofing
10.14 Sail cloth fabric system attached to wall at clerestory
10.16 Steel ladder anchor bolt to floor; fasten to wall/furdown

11 – Equipment

11.02 Ceiling-hung, electric rear-projection screen
11.03 Ceiling-mounted electrical drop down front-projection screen

15 – Mechanical

15.09 Roof drain; re: Plumbing

16 – Electrical

16.02 Scheduled light fixture re: Electrical

KEY NOTES | 1

B/A

BRAVE / ARCHITECTURE

4617 Montrose Blvd., Suite C230
Houston, Texas 77006
Voice: 713.524.5858
Fax: 713.524.5868
studio@bravearchitecture.com
Contact: Fernando Brave

Consultants:

Structural: Matrix Structural Engineers
24 Greenway Plaza
Suite 1508
Houston, Texas 77046-2401
Voice: 713.664.0130
Fax: 713.664.1370
Contact: Chip Hurley

MEP: TGK + Associates
2541 Breaux Trace
Seabrook, Texas 77586
Voice: 832.541.9682
Fax: 281.326.8076
Contact: Thom Kolupski

LEED: Rice & Gardner Consultants, Inc.
6161 Savoy Drive, Suite 1212
Houston, Texas 77036
Voice: 713.482.2300
Fax: 713.482.2314
Contact: James Thornton

SICARDIGALLERY

1506 West Alabama
Houston, TX 77006

Issue:
11/17/10 PERMIT/GMP

B/A Project No.:	07140
Drawn By:	Alp
Checked By:	FLB
CAD File:	07140-A-401.dwg

SECTION DETAILS

Scale: VARIES

A.611

Construction

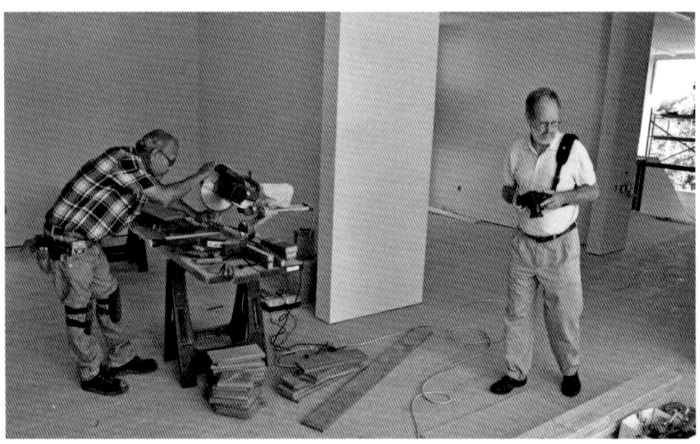

The Building

1506

SICARDI GALLERY
RESERVED
PARKING

SICARDI GALLERY
1506

The tradition of portraiture is one of oldest genres in the
Historically produced for nobility and to represent religious
genre and its subjects have undergone significant change in the past
few centuries. Each artist in this exhibition creates portraits
her unique visual language, whether it is straight forward,
imagined; with an approach that challenges the

Abraham Palatnik: *Progression*

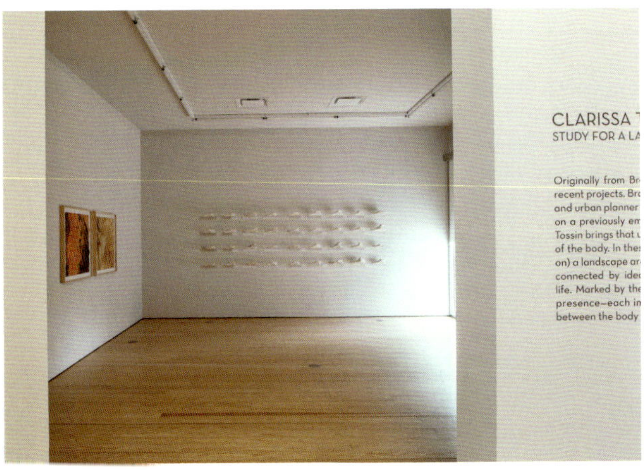
CLARISSA T
STUDY FOR A LA

Progression

....DESFIGURADO
.... PALO DADO
.... LENGUA SUELTA
.....PLOMO
.....A LA CABEZA
.....DOS PIERNAS
.... UN TUNEL
.....PLATA
.....TODAS PARTES
.... AL BULTO

MODERN ART
The Armory Show 2009
SIGNALS
PROSPECT.1

SICARDI GALLERY

SICARDI GALLERY

SICARDI GALLERY

Epilogue Anna Mod

Houston's non-deed restricted areas vividly display the city's development patterns with a cacophonous mix of architectural styles and uses as areas evolve. Case in point are two Montrose streets, Richmond Avenue and West Alabama, both former residential streets changed into major east-to-west thoroughfares with only a smattering of their former use remaining. Most of the front lawns on the segment between Montrose Blvd. and S. Shepherd were long ago concreted over for surface parking to accommodate businesses that now operate in American Foursquare, bungalows, brick clad duplexes, and quadruplexes. Once the deed restrictions expired in the 1960's and were not reinstated, this type of transition happens unchecked and adds another layer onto the city.

Brave / Architecture's two galleries depicted in this book, completed almost a decade apart, are part of the continuum of Houston's ever-changing urban realm. The first, De Santos Gallery on Richmond Ave., now turned into a private office, slyly turns its side to the street yet its massing and scale respect the dominant (formerly) residential set back. When it opened in 2005, the building was the fresh, bold, innovative early twenty-first century newcomer and stood out with its bold façade of stucco punctuated with metal and a thin horizontal window. At the same time, it seemed to co-exist within the scale of the surrounding early twentieth century neighborhood and also demand attention as the young upstart. The building is part of, and a participant with the ever-evolving street, anchored by the Dunlavy Fire Station No.7 from the early 1970's. Across the street, the ubiquitous four-story apartments and townhouses constructed more recently, demonstrate the next likely evolution of the thoroughfare – dense infill built to the property line – with no regard to the

former residential scale and rhythm. The pattern of houses, lawns, apartments, and small commercial strip centers interrupts and repeats as the street moves westward.

Sicardi Gallery, completed in 2014, faces the street with a stuccoed first floor and slightly off-center aluminum framed entry doors and full height glass storefront with a cantilevered, metal-clad second story above. The cantilevered overhang turns the corner formed by the building's main stair to form a glass corner window through which sculptures are exhibited. The result again is a dynamic new building on the street that respects its context and displays an openness and approachability of a commercial building.

Both buildings have been published in Texas Architect and Sicardi recently landed a coveted spot in Phaidon's Destination Architecture (2017) and are part of Houston's legacy of incorporating corrugated metal for art buildings and houses. The trend started with the Art Barn at Rice University (recently demolished) and the tin house movement from 1980's and 90's where metal buildings announced Houston's changing West End, formerly dominated by one-story wood frame cottages. These two gallery buildings occupy a spot in that continuum and demonstrate how a well-designed contemporary building can fit into a street of repurposed revival style houses.

Anna Mod is the Director of the Southwest office of MacRostie Historic Advisors in Houston.

Appendix Biography Firm Profile

Biography
Fernando Brave

Fernando L. Brave, FAIA graduated from the University of Houston with a Master of Architecture in 1988. The year before, he permanently relocated to Houston, Texas after completing his undergraduate architecture studies at the Universidad de Belgrano in Buenos Aires. His professional experience includes the completion of projects for individuals, private companies and public institutions. He has been a key player in large master planning and development projects both in the United States and abroad. His portfolio also includes several pro-bono projects for non-profit institutions in need. In 2002, Fernando founded BRAVE / ARCHITECTURE, an award-winning architecture firm in Houston, Texas.

A Registered Architect and LEED® Accredited Professional, Fernando has lectured on many architectural topics and has written for numerous publications. In 2017, he was invited to the International Architecture Biennial in Buenos Aires as a featured speaker. His works have been recognized with design awards by the Texas Society of Architects, the Houston American Institute of Architects and others, and has been featured in the Houston Chronicle, The Dallas Morning News, Texas Architect, Architectural Record, Wallpaper, and others. Eight of his projects are listed in the third edition of the Houston Architectural Guide, which is published by the Houston AIA.

He has sat on various Boards, such as the Houston Chapter of the American Institute of Architects, the Texas Society of Architects, the Houston Archeological and Historical Commission, the Rice Design Alliance, and those of a few cultural organizations. He is currently a member of the City of Houston's Planning Commission, as appointed by the City's last three Mayors.

Fernando taught design studios at the University of Houston's College of Architecture for ten years, and is a frequent guest juror at several schools of architecture. He has also served as juror for the Design Awards of the American Institute of Architects at different chapters. Outside of his architectural career, his passions include raising a family of six, traveling to the hidden gems around the world, cooking, skiing, sailing, visiting the latest art exhibits, and practicing gratitude for what continues to be a hell of a ride.

In 2012, Fernando was elevated to the College of Fellows of the American Institute of Architects, a program honoring those who have achieved a standard of excellence in the profession and who have made a significant contribution to architecture and society.

Firm Profile

Peter Ho, Alicia Islam, Natasha Dunn, Christian Sheridan, Fernando Brave, Catherine Schoolar, Diana Ngo, Anouk Brave, Rick de la Cruz, Silvana Micolich, Cristina Brown

BRAVE / ARCHITECTURE was founded by Fernando L. Brave, FAIA in Houston, Texas in 2002. Organized as a multi-disciplinary firm, we aim for quality design, innovative technology, and methodical construction detailing. Services range from planning to executing complex architecture and engineering projects. Each design assignment is treated as an opportunity to provide its client with smart solutions, while allowing their unique message its truest expression. BRAVE / ARCHITECTURE's design focuses on cultural, civic, educational, residential, and commercial projects, though from time-to-time, the firm has engaged on other project types based on specific goals or those of its clients.

The firm's practice model translates the energy of the university design studio and the idealized vision of the profession into a successful practice sustaining these paradigms, despite economic pressures and real-world challenges. The firm nurtures the free flow of ideas along architecture's knowledge continuum from education to practice, engaging the community at many levels and showing its commitment to architecture as a social and humanitarian endeavor.

BRAVE / ARCHITECTURE has been successful as a non-traditional practice by turning the traditional model around: not hiring staff based on project needs, but rather seeking project opportunities based on firm resources, capabilities, and ambitions. The firm's staff focus their efforts on a variety of aspects including material research, historical precedents, functionality, and meaning.

The firm's founder steers the firm in elevating the community space — both physical and figurative — into a meaningful, thoughtful, and responsive commonality among people. This commitment rises from their ability to always work with open doors, to invite ideas of others, and to share their own knowledge with generosity and enthusiasm. This working style has resulted in numerous mentions in prestigious publications, as well as many local, state, and national design awards, including multiple AIA Houston Honor Awards, and Texas Society of Architects Design and Studio Awards.

BRAVE / ARCHITECTURE was bestowed the Firm of the Year Award by the American Institute of Architects – Houston Chapter in 2018.

BOOK CREDITS
Art Director: Oscar Riera Ojeda
Graphic Design: Julia Miceli Pitta

PHOTO CREDITS
Fernando Brave: Slip Cover (bottom), Front Cover, Back Cover (left), 13, 15, 16, 68 (bottom), 80, 81, 94, 95, 103, 150, 151,152 (bottom left), 153, 164, 165, 179, 187
Paul Hester: Slip Cover (top), Back Cover (right), 4, 8, 9, 33, 66, 67, 68 (top), 69, 76, 77, 82, 83, 84, 85, 86, 87, 88, 89, 90, 91, 92 (bottom), 93, 96, 97 (top), 97 (bottom), 105, 146, 149, 152 (bottom right), 154, (top), 157, 158, 160, 161, 162, 163, 166, 168, 172, 174, 175, 181, 182, 183, 184
Luis De Santos: 3, 62, 63, 70, 72, 73, 74, 78, 92 (top), 98
Julie Pizzo Wood, c/o Texas Society of Architects: 152 (top),154 (bottom), 155 (bottom), 170 (bottom), 173, 177
Photographs provided by Sicardi Gallery: 154 (top), 155 (top), 156 (top), 160, 161, 170 (top), 171
Rene Magdaleno: 156 (bottom), 167, 178
Houston Chronicle: 190
Anthony Rathbun: 191
Introduction Section Photographs: Unless indicated otherwise, all mages in this section are taken from the Internet. Fig. 1, Paul Hester; Fig. 5, Arend Zweekhorst (Flickr); Fig. 7, Sarath Kuchi (Flickr); Fig. 11, Rice Design Alliance; Fig. 23, Evolvi (Flickr); Fig. 27, Bryan Kelley (Flickr); Fig. 28, Yan Da (Flickr); Fig. 42, Wallpaper* City Guides / Wade Griffith; Figs. 15, 16, 17, 26, 30, 32, 33, and 37, Fernando Brave

All Model and Construction photos in this book are by BRAVE / ARCHITECTURE. Any photography credit errors or omissions are unintentional.

ISBN 978-1-946226-24-2
Published by Oscar Riera Ojeda Publishers Limited
Printed in China

Oscar Riera Ojeda Publishers Limited
Unit 4-6 7/F.,
Far East Consortium Building,
121 Des Voeux Road Central, Hong Kong
T: +852-3920-9312

Production Offices | China
Suite 19, Shenyun Road,
Nanshan District, Shenzhen 518055
T:+86-135-5479-2350

www.oropublishers.com | www.oscarrieraojeda.com
oscar@oscarrieraojeda.com